Tram to Supertram

An Old Friend Returns To The Streets Of Sheffield

The Official Publication about the South Yorkshire Supertram Scheme

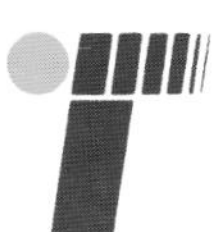

Peter Fox, Paul Jackson and Roger Benton

Published by Platform 5 Publishing Ltd., 3 Wyvern House, Sark Road, Sheffield, S2 4HG in association with South Yorkshire Passenger Executive, Exchange Street, Sheffield, S2 5SZ.

© 1995 Platform 5 Publishing Ltd. No part of this publication may be reproduced or transmitted in any form or by any means electronic, mechanical, photocopying, recording or otherwise, without the prior permission of the publishers. The opinions expressed herein are those of the authors and may not necessarily be those of South Yorkshire PTA or PTE.

ISBN 1 872524 61 3

Printed in England by B.R. Hubbard Printers Ltd., Callywhite Lane, Dronfield, Sheffield, S18 6XP.

Colour Reproduction by Riverside Reprographics, Sheaf Gardens, Duchess Road, Sheffield S2 4BB.

Further copies of this publication may be obtained from Platform 5 Publishing Ltd. at the above address price £4.95. Please add 10% (UK), 20% (Europe) and 30% (rest of world) to cover postage and packing.

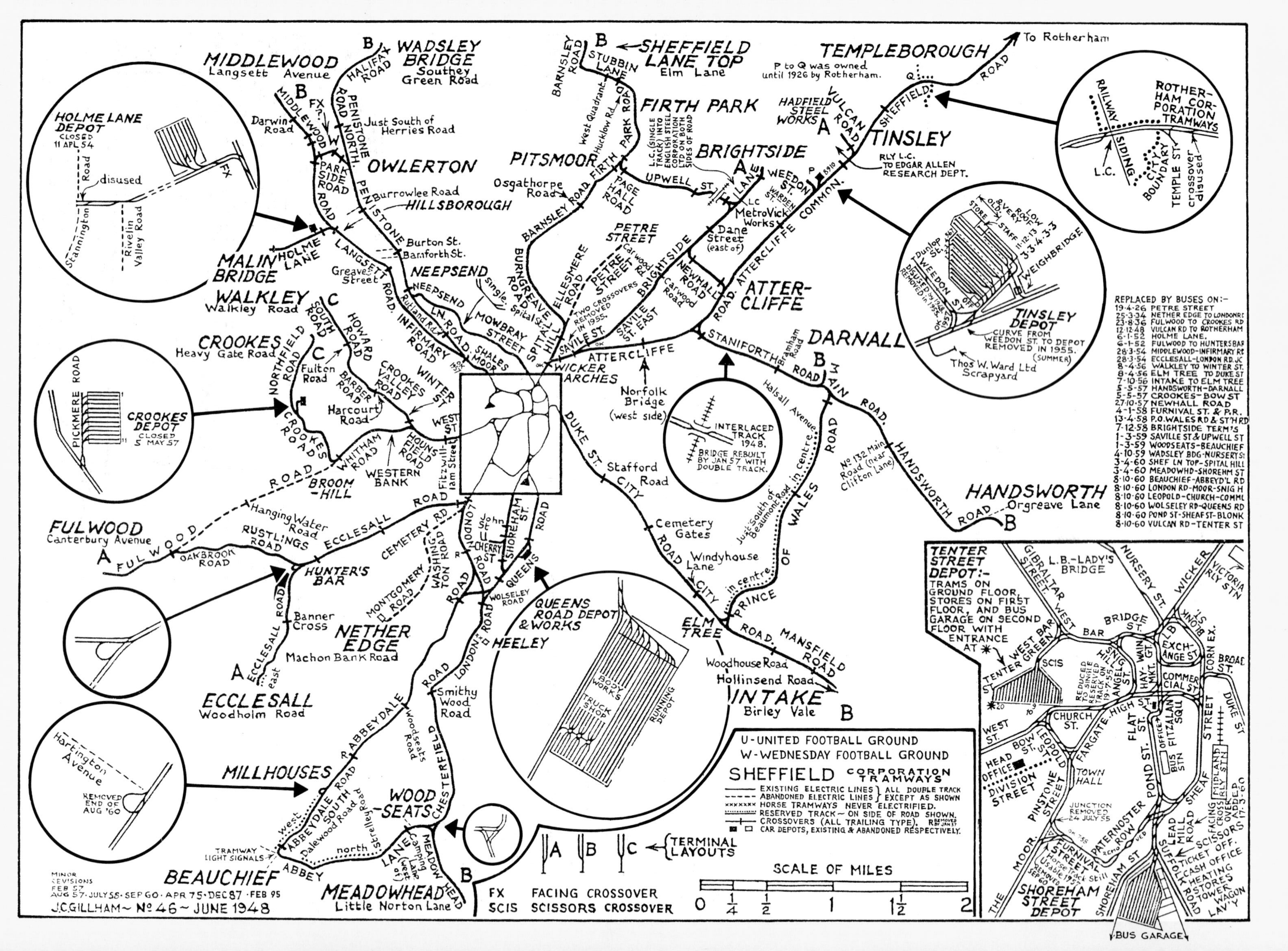
SHEFFIELD CORPORATION TRAMWAYS
U-UNITED FOOTBALL GROUND
W-WEDNESDAY FOOTBALL GROUND
EXISTING ELECTRIC LINES } ALL DOUBLE TRACK
ABANDONED ELECTRIC LINES } EXCEPT AS SHOWN
HORSE TRAMWAYS NEVER ELECTRIFIED.
RESERVED TRACK ~ ON SIDE OF ROAD SHOWN.
CROSSOVERS (ALL TRAILING TYPE).
CAR DEPOTS, EXISTING & ABANDONED RESPECTIVELY.
TERMINAL LAYOUTS
FX FACING CROSSOVER
SCIS SCISSORS CROSSOVER
SCALE OF MILES
0 1/4 1/2 1 1 1/2 2
REPLACED BY BUSES ON:-
19·4·26 PETRE STREET
25·3·34 NETHER EDGE TO LONDON RD
23·8·36 FULWOOD TO CROOKES RD
12·12·48 VULCAN RD TO ROTHERHAM
6·1·52 HOLME LANE.
6·1·52 FULWOOD TO HUNTERSBAR
28·3·54 MIDDLEWOOD-INFIRMARY RD
28·3·54 ECCLESALL-LONDON RD.JC
8·4·56 WALKLEY TO WINTER ST.
8·4·56 ELM TREE TO DUKE ST
7·10·56 INTAKE TO ELM TREE
5·5·57 HANDSWORTH-DARNALL
5·5·57 CROOKES-BOW ST
27·10·57 NEWHALL ROAD
4·1·58 FURNIVAL ST. & P.R.
13·4·58 P.O.WALES RD & ST'H RD
7·12·58 BRIGHTSIDE TERM'S
1·3·59 SAVILLE ST & UPWELL ST
1·3·59 WOODSEATS-BEAUCHIEF
4·10·59 WADSLEY BDG-NURSERY ST
3·4·60 SHEF LN TOP-SPITAL HILL
3·4·60 MEADOWHD-SHOREHM ST
8·10·60 BEAUCHIEF-ABBEYD'L RD
8·10·60 LONDON RD-MOOR-SNIG H
8·10·60 LEOPOLD-CHURCH-COMML
8·10·60 WOLSELEY RD-QUEENS RD
8·10·60 POND ST-SHEAF ST-BLONK
8·10·60 VULCAN RD-TENTER ST
TEMPLEBOROUGH
To Rotherham
P to Q was owned until 1926 by Rotherham.
TINSLEY
RLY L.C. TO EDGAR ALLEN RESEARCH DEPT.
HADFIELD STEEL WORKS
ROTHER-HAM COR-PORATION TRAMWAYS
RAILWAY SIDING
L.C.
CITY BOUNDARY
TEMPLE ST
crossover disused
TINSLEY DEPOT
WEIGHBRIDGE
CURVE FROM WEEDON ST. TO DEPOT REMOVED IN 1955. (SUMMER)
Thos W. Ward Ltd Scrapyard
MIDDLEWOOD
Langsett Avenue
WADSLEY BRIDGE
Southey Green Road
SHEFFIELD LANE TOP
Elm Lane
FIRTH PARK
BRIGHTSIDE
PITSMOOR
OWLERTON
HILLSBOROUGH
NEEPSEND
MALIN BRIDGE
WALKLEY
Walkley Road
CROOKES
Heavy Gate Road
ATTER-CLIFFE
DARNALL
HANDSWORTH
Orgreave Lane
WICKER ARCHES
Norfolk Bridge (west side)
INTERLACED TRACK 1948. BRIDGE REBUILT BY JAN 57 WITH DOUBLE TRACK.
HOLME LANE DEPOT
CLOSED 11 APL 54
CROOKES DEPOT
CLOSED 5 MAY 57
FULWOOD
Canterbury Avenue
BROOM-HILL
HUNTER'S BAR
NETHER EDGE
ECCLESALL
Woodholm Road
HEELEY
QUEENS ROAD DEPOT & WORKS
BODY WORKS
TRUCK SHOP
RUNNING DEPOT
ELM TREE
INTAKE
Birley Vale
MILLHOUSES
WOOD-SEATS
BEAUCHIEF
MEADOWHEAD
Little Norton Lane
Hartington Avenue
REMOVED END OF AUG '60
TRAMWAY LIGHT SIGNALS
TENTER STREET DEPOT:- TRAMS ON GROUND FLOOR, STORES ON FIRST FLOOR, AND BUS GARAGE ON SECOND FLOOR WITH ENTRANCE AT
L.B.-LADY'S BRIDGE
HEAD OFFICE
SHOREHAM STREET DEPOT
BUS GARAGE
MINOR REVISIONS FEB 57 AUG 57·JULY 58·SEP 60·APR 75·DEC 87·FEB 95
J.C.GILLHAM ~ No 46 ~ JUNE 1948

Sheffield's Former Trams: 87 Years of Service

THE HORSE TRAM ERA

The original Sheffield horse tramway routes were constructed under the 1870 Tramways Act, the powers being granted in July 1872, the routes to Attercliffe and Carbrook, Brightside, Heeley, Nether Edge and Owlerton opening progressively between 1873 and 1877. Under the legislation at that time local authorities were expressly precluded from actually operating tramways but they were empowered to construct them and lease the lines to an individual or an operating company. In this case the tracks were constructed by contractors for the Corporation and leased to the Sheffield Tramways Company who operated the initial services.

Prior to this date primitive horse buses had provided a limited public service but road surfaces at that time were of poor quality and their carrying capacity was quite small. The new horse trams, giving a smooth ride on their steel rails provided a considerable improvement over the transport facilities which had previously been provided in the town. However the fares charged were still much higher than the ordinary working man could afford so horse trams were of very limited use to him, encouraging him to continue living as close as he could to his place of employment, walking to and from work each day. Services would not, in any case have begun each day until well after the ordinary artisan should have started work. The great cost to the tramway operator of keeping a large number of horses in stock meant that he could not offer low fares.

The initial powers had been granted for routes from a town loop round Blonk Street, the Norfolk Market Hall in Exchange Street and Waingate to Carbrook and to Brightside, with additional routes to Heeley, Nether Edge and Hillsborough. In horse car days there was an inconvenient gap in services in the stretch of roads between Exchange Street and the Moorhead which continued until preparations were in hand for electrification of the system in 1898/1899. In the event the loop line was not a success and the terminus for the East End cars became Lady's Bridge. The loop line was subsequently lifted. The Heeley and Nether Edge routes operated in isolation from the rest, having their own depots at Albert Road, Heeley and at Nether Edge terminus. The trams operating to the East End and to Hillsborough used Tinsley depot (at Carbrook terminus), a small depot at Brightside next to the Bridge Inn (1885-1900 only) and a depot built in Holme Lane, Hillsborough. There was a connecting line between the Hillsborough (Snig Hill) and East End (Lady's Bridge) routes which was used to get trams to the workshop facilities provided by the company at Tinsley depot.

It was commonplace in those days for cars to carry differing colours to denote each route operated in addition to carrying the name of the actual route. In this way the illiterate as well as the educated could identify easily the tram they needed. A surviving Sheffield horse tram carries the Brightside red route colour and lettering.

STEAM TRAMS

The company claimed from time to time that it was making insufficient profits. In 1876 and also in 1878 trials were carried out with steam tram-engines which, by eliminating the requirement for horses, had the potential for providing additional company profits. They were to become used in considerable numbers in other areas of the country but concerns were expressed that these vehicles would frighten horses and could be dangerous. In areas where they were brought into use, the operators had to accept stringent operating regulations necessitating arrangements for engines to consume their own smoke and for the 'motion' to be completely covered as near to the road surface as was possible. The steam tram-engines found no favour here with the town council and the idea went no further in Sheffield.

Facing Page: A map of the former Sheffield Corporation Tramways courtesy of Mr. J.C. Gillham. The map has been modified by us with Mr. Gillham's permission to better fit the modern A4 page size.

Right: A double-deck horse tram at Nether Edge depot at the turn of the century. Two horses were needed because of the weight of these vehicles. The shell of this building on Machon Bank Road still exists and is used as a part of a car showroom *National Tramway Museum*

ELECTRIC OPERATION

In July 1896 Sheffield Corporation, who had frequently locked swords with the Sheffield Tramways Company, took over the undertaking, being one of the first few local councils to become authorised to operate tramways. They decided to expand and mechanise the system.

Almost immediately a committee was formed to inspect other tramways in this country and abroad to look at the improved systems of traction then becoming available with a view to advising the full council appropriately on which of them they should adopt. On their return they recommended the adoption of electrical propulsion using the overhead current collection system.

In those days there was no national electricity supply available and few existing local suppliers were capable of providing the current required for expanding electric tramways. Often there was little alternative but for tramway operators to provide their own power supply. The supply industry itself was in its infancy and opportunities were identified for the tramway industry to become local domestic and industrial electricity supplier where the additional load could become commercially and financially useful. Many of them did but, as an alternative, some local authorities set up their own Electricity Supply Department, thus becoming able to sell current cheaply but profitably to their own Tramway Department. A power station was constructed for the Sheffield Corporation Tramways Department at Kelham Island by the River Don between Mowbray Street and Alma Street - now used as the Kelham Island Industrial Museum. Feeder cables from here provided current to the extremities of the system, eventually covering well over forty miles of route.

Above: A contemporary postcard view of Nether Edge tram terminus ca. 1910. The tram depicted is of the same type as the one shown on the back cover of this book. *Courtesy National Tramway Museum*

The horse tram routes continued to operate but now under the control of the council and with various improvements put in hand, particularly as the old tracks were gradually reconstructed with heavier rail in anticipation of the electric services to come. The Walkley, Hunters Bar and Abbeydale routes were constructed and horse cars were provided temporarily. The missing link between Moorhead and Lady's Bridge was laid in and at long last all the routes became connected together.

Public operation of the initial electric routes to Nether Edge and Tinsley was to commence on 6th September 1899 with the Walkley route opening 18th September and Pitsmoor on 27th September. Two trams survive from this early electric period; Number 46, a single deck 'Walkley' car in use from the opening of that route in 1899 and a double-deck car number 74 of 1900 but preserved as rebuilt with a covered top deck in 1909 (see back cover).

The electric car routes opened progressively in the early years of this century allowing the last horse car service on the Hillsborough route to be withdrawn in November 1902.

Left: Fitzalan Square c. 1900 with an open-topped double decker. Haymarket is in the background. On the left is the cabman's shelter, well-known to older Sheffield people. *Courtesy National Tramway Museum*

Above Right: The junction of Ecclesall Road with the Moor c. 1905. *Courtesy National Tramway Museum*

Below Right: Fitzalan Square looking down Commercial Street showing the gas offices c.1910. *Courtesy National Tramway Museum*

Services were provided along the following roads out of the city:

Burngreave Road and Barnsley Road.
Ellesmere Road and Petre Street.
Savile Street and Brightside Lane,
Attercliffe Road and Attercliffe Common.
Staniforth Road and Main Road.
Duke Street, City Road and Mansfield Road,
The Moor, London Road and Chesterfield Road.
Cemetery Road, Washington Road, Wostenholm Road, Montgomery Road and Moncreiffe Road,
Ecclesall Road, Rustlings Road and Oakbrook Road,
West Street, Glossop Road, Hounsfield Road, Western Bank, Whitham Road and Fulwood Road,
Winter Street, Crookes Valley Road, Barber Road, Commonside, Howard Road and South Road,
Crookes Road and Crookes,
West Bar, Gibraltar Street, Shalesmoor, Infirmary Road, Langsett Road and Holme Lane,
Penistone Road, Nursery Street, Mowbray Street and Neepsend Lane.

By 1905 the basic system was in place and later developments extended these routes out of the city or, by providing connecting lines, circular or cross country services were created. However, although there had been several proposals for other services, no further main roads out of the city were provided with tramway services.

In 1905 the Rotherham Corporation tramway line to Tinsley was connected with the Sheffield system and through running began between the two operators. However it was not always a harmonious arrangement, ill feeling between them coming to the surface from time to time, even causing discontinuation of the through services from September 1914 to May 1915. The real losers, of course, were the passengers who were forced to change cars at Tinsley during this period, although some perhaps preferred instead to use the competing railway services which must have reduced the income to both of the tramway operators.

From this time until the end of the Great War in 1918 the tramcar was undoubtedly the fastest and most efficient public service vehicle on the city streets. Sheffield Corporation Tramways Department put on motor bus services to connect with the outlying tram termini, runningto Lodge Moor, Rivelin Valley, Wincobank and Totley with additional services to Upperthorpe and Heeley Green. A few private bus operators had also come on the scene. However the vehicles used were primitive and had to contend with the rough road surfaces of the period, comparing very unfavourably with the speed and comfort provided by the electric tramcars.

Left: Car No. 131 at Staniforth Road, Darnall c. 1915. This car is the same type as the preserved car shown on the back cover.
Courtesy National Tramway Museum

Below: Fitzalan Square in 1913 with a both single-deck and double-deck cars in evidence.
Courtesy National Tramway Museum

Bottom: The beautifully finished interior of preserved car No. 74 at the National Tramway Museum. *Peter Fox*

The war of 1914-1918 had been a turning point in several respects. Equipment became scarce, new track-work became less easily obtainable and by 1918 most British tramway systems were suffering from low investment and deferred maintenance. Many smaller systems took the easy way out and closed down as soon as possible because to replace worn equipment and to buy new cars for the extended services, which by then had become necessary, would have been prohibitively expensive. Instead they chose to scrap the lot and buy new buses instead. By this date bus technology had improved. Throughout the country, small bus operators began to work on routes in competition with the trams. Large, efficient tramway operators like Sheffield, whilst troubled by these developments, did not consider seriously the possibility of wholesale replacement of

the trams at this stage but did begin to expand their own bus operations, often to beat off this competition. Trolley buses had been considered, but did not in the event find favour in Sheffield, motor buses being much preferred by the City Council.

Because of wartime shortages, twenty second hand double-deck trams were purchased from the London County Council Tramways in 1917/18, an unusual course for the tramway department to take at that time but which had become necessary in order to provide the required services in Sheffield and also to replace a number of single deck trams, some of which were sold to other operators.

EXPANSION AND DEVELOPMENT

Reflecting the growing importance of the motorbus in the Sheffield fleet the title of the transport department had been changed to SHEFFIELD CORPORATION TRAMWAYS AND MOTORS during the Great War and considerable improvements to the services and also to the tram and bus fleets were begun after the hostilities were over. Notwithstanding the difficulties resulting from deferred maintenance during the war and in the period immediately following this the emergence of the modern day scourge of inflation, the tramway services were to be extended and the fleet was to be modernised and augmented, incorporating many new innovations and improvements. Powerful air and magnetic braking systems were adopted. Until this time drivers and passengers alike had to endure the harshness of open balcony and open platform cars even during inclement winter weather. Tramcars in the existing fleet were improved by fully or partially enclosing them and cars of new designs were ordered from several manufacturers. Significantly the large overhaul works owned by the department and situated on Queens Road had proved itself capable of building trams and buses, providing work for skilled Sheffield workmen. (This building was demolished in 1993).

The 1920s heralded increased activity for the tramways but also brought about the first major abandonment. It had been proposed to extend the Petre Street service to Grimesthorpe and beyond, but rather than incur the considerable expense of renewing the track, which had become necessary, and providing the capital expenditure to extend the tramway route, motor buses were purchased instead and the short tram route closed down in April 1925. During this decade the designs of motorbuses were becoming much improved and increasingly more attractive to tramway operators and passengers alike but the trams in Sheffield were to remain the mainstay of public transport and would still have a further life of over thirty years ahead of them.

New trams continued to be built, with building programmes being instituted in order to replace older cars which were scrapped. Most of these new cars were constructed in the Queens Road Works using local skilled labour wherever possible.

Short extensions of established routes were constructed together with two major lines linking services together. Tracks were constructed and opened in 1927 along Abbey Lane against local opposition. A long length of reserved track grassed and landscaped between Strelley Road and Dalewood Road was to prove very popular and provided access to particularly pleasant scenery. Prince of Wales Road line linked the Handsworth and Intake routes together, producing not only a new frequent service for the Manor estate but also opportunities for direct peak hour works services to and from the East End and Intake.

Right: No. 121, a 1928 standard car on the grassed reservation at the side of Abbey Lane in 1958.
Frank Hunt Collection courtesy LRTA

Below: Prince of Wales Road looking towards Darnall in the late 1940s. The photograph was probably taken in the evening rush hour judging by the number of trams in evidence. Note the absence of motor vehicles! *A.D. Packer*

THE 1930s

A 1928 standard car in old livery at Sheffield Lane Top terminus. The trolley is being turned round by the automatic trolley reverser watched by a member of the maintenance staff on the tower wagon which is now preserved at the National Tramway Museum — *Bernard Mettam*

The tramways still seemed to have a certain future in Sheffield, extensions being built along Mansfield Road to the city boundary, Handsworth Road to Orgreave Lane and also Stubbin Lane and Barnsley Road to Sheffield Lane Top. Against this the Nether Edge Route was to close in March 1934 in the face of the cost of track renewals. For similar reasons the Nether Green via Broomhill route closed in August 1936. A new tramway extension was proposed and powers were obtained to extend the Sheffield Lane Top route through the Shiregreen housing estate around Hartley Brook Road, Nether Shire Lane and Sicey Avenue but in the event a new bus service commenced instead.

Things settled down now and before the Second World War commenced in 1939 the department had gained a just reputation for efficiency, low fares, comfort and cleanliness of the vehicles. It is true to say that Sheffield people generally liked their tram services which they considered to be regular and reliable. The old colour scheme of Prussian blue with cream bands with gold leaf lining began to give way to a scheme of cream with azure blue bands, contrasting starkly with some of the smoke-infested, grimy areas in the city, particularly in the East End. The platform staff rightly considered themselves fortunate to be in such well respected jobs and were proud of the positions they held. There were a number of social activities and a staff magazine was produced. The staff social club at Four Lane Ends, Meadowhead (known locally as the 'Tramways Club') provided sports and games activities for all departmental staff. The Transport Department, dominated by the tramway staff who were in the majority, seemed to be a progressive, happy organisation with a continuing and bright future. The fleet had increased to over 450 trams.

In 1936, a new improved design of tram was introduced. These had a more sleek appearance than previous designs and were generally known as 'domed roof' cars. One of these, No. 251 is seen at the top of Angel Street on a special working in 1958. — *Bernard Mettam*

THE SECOND WORLD WAR AND ITS AFTERMATH

The Sheffield tramway system entered the 1939-45 war in good shape, maintenance having been second to none for a number of years. The virtual elimination of private motoring and the non-essential use of fuel oils as a result of wartime restrictions did however over-stretch capacity on the tramcars which inevitably bore the greatest load. Bus services were curtailed, especially in the late evening, throwing much extra loading on the trams. Tramcars had to have their lighting drastically subdued in wartime in order not to become visible to enemy raiders overhead but otherwise their performance remained impeccable, although measures had to be taken to avoid, as far as possible, any unnecessary flashing from the overhead wires when setting points or when trolleys were passing under section-insulators.

Road vehicles were given coats of white paint along protruding edges to help pedestrians and other road users to indentify them during the 'blackout' and trams were no exception. Collision fenders on tramcars were painted white. A small slit in a headlamp mask allowed a limited downward facing light for the benefit of the driver. Later in the war when repainting became necessary, and as paint supplies became difficult to obtain, trams and buses were given a grey livery. The name 'Sheffield' was removed from the sides of trams and buses and this, together with other road traffic measures which were introduced, was hoped to 'confuse the enemy'.

As had happened in the Great War women were again taken on as tram conductors to replace the men who had been 'called up' and, although for security reasons Sheffield was not referred to directly, it was obvious that a book by Zelma Katin published in 1944 entitled 'CLIPPIE - the Autobiography of a Wartime Conductress' was set in Sheffield. It describes vividly her training and experiences in Steel City, conducting on the yellow and blue double deckers.

Air raids on the city brought tremendous problems for the tramway system, overhead equipment and to the street track. It suffered not only from direct hits on tramcars and track, the overhead wires were often left with no support owing to damage to some buildings to which the wires were attached. Fires spread to trams which had been left in the city centre during raids in December 1940 and several were burnt out completely. Fortunately Queens Road Works was gradually able to replace some of these with newly built tramcars using as much of the original equipment as had survived, together with body parts either held in stock or which still could be made even with the restrictions then in force. Nevertheless there was the loss of a number of irreplaceable trams due to enemy action and a heavy demand for rush hour transport caused the department to look around for second hand ones from other towns and cities.

In the event help was forthcoming from the cities of Newcastle and Bradford. A total of twenty-four second hand trams were purchased from these sources and, after considerable modification, proved very useful mainly during peak hours. They survived in Sheffield for about ten years and one of the ex-Bradford cars was later converted into a departmental vehicle, eventually passing into preservation in 1960.

Considering the general wartime shortages of materials, equipment, skilled labour, the war damage and the overloading, particularly during rush hours when munition workers had to be transported to and from work, the tramways had coped surprisingly well. However, once more neglect had occurred and maintenance had suffered during the Second World War as it had done during the Great War. Prices had begun to escalate again as they had done after 1918. Inflation again had begun again to affect the tramway finances.

The Transport Department began to address the problem of an ageing fleet of tramcars which would need gradual replacement and in 1946 unveiled the first post-war new tramcar number 501, built in Queens Road Works and intended to be a prototype for a new fleet of modern trams to be built there. It incorporated new refinements including more powerful motors and fluorescent lighting. In the event thirty-five further trams based on that prototype design were ordered from Charles Roberts & Co of Wakefield which were to be the last new 'traditional' British trams to be delivered to the city.

In 1948 a new bridge was built over the railway on Sheffield Road between Vulcan Road and Bawtry Road at Tinsley. In order to enable the work to be done the through tram route between Rotherham and Sheffield was temporarily suspended. However it was decided not to reinstate the through tram service and a replacement bus service was substituted thus being the first route to be closed after the war. Rotherham council decided very shortly after this to discontinue their tram service (which had been curtailed to Templeborough) in 1949. The new Supertram route to Meadowhall passes under this rebuilt bridge.

Right: The prototype tram No. 501 buit at Queens Road Works in 1946 seen in Commercial Street near to the site of the Supertram Fitzalan Square/Ponds Forge stop. This tram was the basis of the 35 cars built by Charles Roberts from 1948 onwards.
National Tramway Museum

THE 1950s

Above: The Roberts cars were a development of the prototype 501 shown on the previous page, but had an all metal body structure and tungsten lighting. Gandy in his book 'Sheffield Corporation Tramways' describes them as 'probably the only really good thingwhich happened in Sheffield urban transport since 1939'. This description was probably appropriate at the time he wrote his book, but is clearly now incorrect! *Bernard Mettam*

In 1951, even before the last of the thirty-five new Sheffield tramcars was delivered the City Council had decided that a programme of substitution by motorbuses for the whole tramway fleet should be instituted. The decision was not unanimous, Councillor R.W. Allott resigning from the ruling Labour Group in protest. Comparing the cost of replacement trams with the cost at that time of simply buying new buses, which were far cheaper, the decision seemed logical based upon substituting like with like. However the life-span of a tramcar would have been considerably longer than that of a motorbus and a modern continental tramcar carried far more passengers, but the trend in public passenger transport had been away from the tramcar in this country since the 1930s when development of tramway equipment here had all-but ceased. This made the remaining vehicles appear to be quaint and antiquated in comparison with the modern buses in production. It is true to say that in areas in this country where trams remained in use, some attempt had been made to apply 'streamlining' to improve the bodywork but the type of electrical and mechanical equipment in use remained the same and, with a few notable exceptions, the production of modern trams in this country had ceased.

An experiment in Sheffield lasting only five months in 1952 with a new tram and bus livery of green (or two tone green) was not popular with Sheffield residents and politicians alike. The cream and blue colour scheme for buses and trams was popular and notwithstanding the possible cost-savings that could be anticipated by the change, the new colour scheme was utterly disliked and the experiment was terminated very quickly, the vehicles concerned being repainted cream and blue.

Traffic congestion in Sheffield was partly blamed on the trams but there were in fact few attempts to promote modern traffic management schemes incorporating them. The politicians and planners at that time saw no future in tramways in this country and promoted projects which catered ex-

Left: The former Sheffield trams had very comfortable 2 + 1 seating and were very popular with passengers. This is a view of the lower saloon of 510 preserved at Crich, but comfortable seats were also provided in the earlier (1928 and 1936) designs of trams also. It is not surprising that passengers regarded the buses which replaced the trams as inferior. *Peter Fox*

Above: The type of tram shown above were nicknamed 'rocker panels' and were charcterised by their lower bodysides which sloped inwards and their banjo-shaped lower front window panes which were designed to allow for their large brake handles. They had longitudinal bench seats on the lower deck. They were built between 1919 and 1927 by Brush or Cravens and similar vehicles were rebuilt by Sheffield Corporation from open balcony cars. They gradually disappeared in the 50s, although three lasted until 1957. No. 457 is seen at Woodseats.

Frank Hunt Collection courtesy LRTA

Above: The first of the tram routes remaining in the 1950s to be closed was that between Fulwood and Malin Bridge. This photograph shows 'domed roof' car 249 on Holme Lane on 20th March 1954, two years after services had been withdrawn, and one week before withdrawal of services between Ecclesall and Middlewood. The road was still used by trams to get to the depot and this car has crossed over to run on the wrong side of the road to run into the depot connection which can be seen in the foreground. *R.J.S. Wiseman*

Right: The trams were blamed for traffic congestion in Sheffield, but was it the trams which got in the way of the cars, or was it the cars which got in the way of the trams? High Street on 18th December 1954.

Courtesy National Tramway Museum

Above: Fitzalan Square in 1954. Soldiers were a common sight in town in those days of National Service (known to Americans as 'draft').

Frank Hunt Collection courtesy LRTA

clusively for motor transport in the city, often to the disadvantage of pedestrians, whom they frequently banished to subways and dank areas underground. We shall see later how this state of affairs did not occur in many cities in the rest of Europe and how events there eventually were to influence our more enlightened decision-making some thirty-five years later, although some countries made the same mistakes as Britain, notably France.

The first route conversion was Fulwood-Malin Bridge in January 1952 to be followed by enormous public protests about the tram scrapping scheme. Sheffield folk were fond of their trams and did not take kindly to the prospect of losing them. A petition circulated amongst the residents and traders of Holme Lane was submitted to the City Council in an unsuccessful attempt to get their route reinstated. It was more than two years before the next route conversion (Ecclesall-Middlewood) took place in March 1954. A further two years were to elapse before the conversion programme was to begin in earnest, gathering momentum until two route closures per year were achieved. Messrs T.W. Ward received the majority of the trams for scrapping via a track connection into their scrap-yard on Attercliffe Common almost opposite the end of Weedon Street. This was on a site immediately adjacent to the new Carbrook Supertram stop - now occupied by the Meadowhall Retail Park.

The final route from Beauchief to Vulcan Road closed on the afternoon of Saturday 8th October 1960. An illuminated car, followed by a procession of fourteen trams carrying specially booked passengers and guests of the City Council set out from Tenter Street Depot on that very wet evening for a final run to Beauchief and back to the city centre. Dignitaries and their honoured guests, having ridden on number 510, the decorated official last tram, then repaired to the Town Hall for a ceremony to mark the occasion, whilst those privileged to hold appropriate tickets rode on cars bound for Tinsley Depot or to Queens Road Works. Trams setting out for the latter point were some of those destined later for preservation.

Right: The last route to be withdrawn was that from Beauchief to Vulcan Road (Tinsley) on 8th October 1960. This photograph was taken in 1954 on the reserved track which ran between Beauchief and Millhouses. The road was converted to a dual carriageway once the tramway was closed. Perhaps one day we will see the process reversed and Supertrams will run where only road vehicles are seen now! *Frank Hunt Collection courtesy LRTA*

PRESERVATION

Local members of the Tramway Museum Society, a national voluntary organisation set up in 1955, are proud to have played their part in the setting up of the National Tramway Museum at Crich. A stone building at Crich, at what eventually was to become the tramway museum site was being considered in 1958/9 as a possible temporary home for a Sheffield tramcar which had been generously donated to the society by the Sheffield City Council. At that time no museum devoted to tramcar history existed anywhere in the country and museums of industrial archaeology had yet to gain general acceptance in many quarters of the main museum movement. There were however several small groups which had taken possession of tramcars and associated historical equipment from tramway operators which was stored in temporary accommodation around the country in the hope that eventually they could be gathered together and operated at some unspecified date in the future at premises as yet to be identified.

Above: No. 330 is preserved at the National Tramway Museum in its final form as a single-deck works car. It was part of a batch which had been bought from Bradford as a temporary replacement for trams damaged in the war. It is seen in 1960 rounding the curve from Abbey Lane to Meadowhead which was normally only used by school trams. *R.J.S. Wiseman*

Below: No. 513 in the centenary procession at Blackpool on 29th August 1985. It had been on loan to the Blackpool & Fleetwood Tramway for the summer. *Paul Jackson*

The Crich site, only twenty-five miles from the city, intended initially to be a temporary home for just one Sheffield tramcar, was recognized to be such a promising property that a decision was quickly made for the whole tramway museum movement to embrace it. One by one the trams in preservation were moved to the premises which were at first leased and then purchased for the purpose of creating the National Tramway Collection.

Very fortunately sufficient vehicles and equipment had been saved or remained in existence at that time to enable a logical collection policy to be adopted and the preservation of additional important items including full size tramcars of varying types commenced. Inevitably the sources of many items were to be those tramway systems which had survived until the late 1950s including Leeds, Glasgow, Blackpool and, of course, Sheffield.

PRESERVED SHEFFIELD TRAMCARS

National Tramway Museum, Crich, Derbyshire.

No. 15. Horse tram built by Starbuck of Birkenhead in 1874. Displayed in Brightside livery of red and cream.

No. 46. Single deck electric car built by G.F. Milnes 1899 for the opening of the system. Ran usually on Walkley route.

No. 74. Built at Electric Railway, Tramway and Carriage Works, Preston in 1900. The car carries a short top cover of distinctive design.

No. 189. Built by Sheffield Corporation Transport Department 1934.

No. 264. Built by Sheffield Corporation Transport Department 1937.

No. 330. Bought by Sheffield Transport Department from Bradford during the last war after several Sheffield trams had received 'blitz' damage. When it became surplus to requirements it was converted in the early 1950s to a rail-grinder.

No. 510. Thirty-five of these cars were built by Charles Roberts & Co Ltd of Horbury, Wakefield. This was Sheffield's official last tramcar (but the new Supertrams now deny it that title).

North of England Open Air Museum, Beamish Hall, Beamish, Co. Durham

No. 513. A further example of a 'Roberts' car although some original control equipment has been replaced by second-hand material from Blackpool owing to unfortunate thefts from the car some years ago whilst in store.

No. 264 (of the old numbering series). Built by United Electric Car Co., Preston. Formerly in the care of the British Transport Commission at Clapham Museum, London (now closed).

Sheffield Bus Museum, Former Tinsley Tram Depot, Sheffield.

No. 460. Built Cravens 1926. Only the lower saloon remains, but a top deck is available.

COPY

Tramway Abandonment 'Facts' or Fallacies

Many reasons were expounded in the early 1950s to justify the closure of the Sheffield tramway system. Unfortunately a large number can be seen to have been one sided and without substance. At the time the "Sheffield Tramways Development Association" attempted to bring these deficiencies to the fore but the elected members would not entertain any change to their decision, and as has been seen, the system closed in 1960. A few points will no doubt interest our 1990s readers:

"Trams are noisy"

The old trams which served Sheffield extremely well over many years, could justifiably have been accused of being noisy. However that does not mean that all cars had to be that way. As mentioned earlier an American design had been produced 20 years before the demise of the Sheffield tram which was very quiet. Rubber inserts on the wheels and better springing cut down the noise level very effectively. The ultimate test now is to compare the old trams with the new "Supertram", and judge for yourself.

Although it is quite obvious that many mistakes were made in abandoning the old tramway system, it is only right to record the words in 1960, of the Chairman of Sheffield Transport Department:

He stated that "... modern conditions demand a change in our mode of public transport." It could be said that modern conditions in the 1990s demand a new mode - SUPERTRAM.

"Trams are more obstructive"

This argument can easily be dispelled when one realises that road users can always predict the path of a tram. Properly sited loading islands as mentioned earlier also prevent the highly obstructive movements created by buses moving into and out from curb edges to pick up or set down passengers. However the main cause of obstruction on our roads today is brought about not by the public service vehicle, but by the never ending stream of private cars, which are responsible for untold damage as well.

"Trams are obsolete"

Mitigating circumstances created this impression. Unfortunately Sheffield together with the last few remaining systems in the UK were at a stage where replacement vehicles and infrastructure was necessary. This led to a belief that nothing "new" was possible in the field of tramways. However at the time Sheffield was closing its celebrated system, cities throughout mainland Europe and North America were steadily updating their fleets with new vehicles and modernising their facilities. The advancement of technology had, 20 years earlier, provided a superbly quiet and speedy tram across the Atlantic, and the introduction of the articulated vehicle was well under way in Europe. Unfortunately these developments were never even considered.

"Problems are caused by picking up and setting down passengers in the centre of roadways"

Just because Sheffield had always operated in this fashion there was no reason to presume that this was an absolute necessity. With a little imagination, special passenger loading islands like those provided outside the Town Hall and by the junction of Fargate and Church Street, segregated from other traffic, could have been constructed at other points on the system. Incidentally, central islands have always been regarded as aids to traffic flow, and even roads without the operation of tramways have been generously provided with such items.

"Buses are cheaper than trams"

In 1951 it was stated that new double deck trams would cost £7,300 each against £4,000 for each new bus, which at the time carried fewer passengers. Of course the life expectancy of each mode was conveniently ignored - 30 years being an accepted life of a tram, 12 for a bus. Using the official figures therefore, it is obvious that more buses were required to cover the life expectancy of new trams, and therefore the cost proved to be much higher.

The "Statement of estimated annual expenses" claimed that buses would be cheaper to run, but to justify these remarks the costs conveniently did not provide for adjustments, and upkeep of highways for bus operation. Up to the time of closing, the tramways were not only responsible for the maintenance of the track and foundations but the 1870 Tramways Act made the tramway accountable for the upkeep of the roadway between the rails and up to 18" either side. When buses took over these costs were no longer the direct responsibility of the Transport Department. However they were the liability of the City Council and ultimately the ratepayer.

It should be noted that existing assets such as vehicles, infrastructure, overhead cabling, sub stations etc. with a book value in excess of £2.3 million were wilfully destroyed by the decision to abandon the Sheffield system. At no time did the Council consult with its ratepayers (i.e. THE OWNERS) before they destroyed assets of its citizens.

"Buses will attract more passengers, by being more flexible"

Unfortunately this claim never materialised, and it has been proven over many years that buses do not attract motorists, who in the main consider the mode as an inferior form of transport. Experience from abroad and reproduced recently in Manchester, has shown that tramways have the ability to entice people from their cars which in turn cuts congestion and in time will re-humanise our city centres.

"Trams are slow"

Had the local authorities invested in really modern trams possessing greater acceleration than any other form of road transport, with the ability to move away from stopping places much more easily than competitors, then this accusation would have been seen to be totally untrue. Vehicles were available but the reliance on tried and conventional methods held sway. In conjunction with speed it has to be stressed that the braking systems employed on trams are far more effective than motor vehicles. Together the attributes of speed and powerful braking result in a quicker and safer operation.

"Whilst at roundabouts, the trams had to have special arrangements made and they could not always flow with other traffic"

It was entirely incorrect to claim that special arrangements were necessary at roundabouts. Many examples, even at that time, were available to show that trams could negotiate such facilities in the same way as motor traffic, Amsterdam being a classic example. However it is quite obvious that tramways, and buses for that matter, should be segregated wherever possible, to provide efficient, safe and reliable transportation.

The caption to this photograph (right) of the roundabout at the junction between the Moor and Ecclesall Road from Sheffield Transport Department's 1960 publication 'The Tramway Era in Sheffield' read:

"could not always flow with other traffic"

It implied that this was a disadvantage of tramways.

Below: The new extension of the tramway in Nantes, France has, however been built with the tramway cutting through roundabouts in the same way as was derided in the 1960s! In this case the tram is given priority. All road traffic lights go red whilst the tram passes through.
Peter Fox

WHY LIGHT RAIL?

The South Yorkshire Supertram System is an example of a Light Rail system (often called Light Rail Transit systems or LRT). Other Light Rail systems in the United Kingdom are the Tyne & Wear Metro in Newcastle, the Docklands Light Railway in London and the Manchester Metrolink system.

All these systems are different from one another but all have the characteristic of being railways which are operated by versatile vehicles which can negotiate sharp curves and steep gradients not normally associated with conventional trains. To some extent the Tyne and Wear Metro and the Docklands Light Railway are unusual in that they are fully segregated systems, unlike those in Manchester and Sheffield which are operated by trams. A tram is a particular type of light rail vehicle which can operate on-street, as well as on segregated track. Thus trams have to be able to stop much faster than ordinary rail vehicles and as far as street running is concerned, they must have many of the characteristics of ordinary road vehicles.

Traditional railways generally rely on rigorous segregation from people and from other vehicles because the train's combination of speed and weight coupled with lack of emergency braking mean that its movement must generally be protected and constrained by formalised signalling systems. Light rail vehicles, conversely, can run on-sight like road vehicles when circumstances permit and this is what permits them to do their unique job.

Light rail vehicles impose less axle load on track and bridges than do some heavy trains, and this means that new structures can be fashioned less substantially, more inexpensively and perhaps with more built-in stylishness and delicacy as well.

THE CONVENTIONAL RAIL ALTERNATIVE

For fast journeys between centres of population and for moving heavy flows of passengers around in large densely-populated conurbations, conventional railway technology will always have an unchallenged edge over all other forms of land transport.

Where short conventional rail journeys are concerned, though, the access times at each end of the ride can represent a high proportion of the total door-to-door travel time. Conventional railways do not always penetrate suburbs well, but the Altrincham line in Greater Manchester where it passes through Sale was a notable exception. This line has now been converted to light rail operation as part of the Manchester Metrolink system. People who wish to use conventional railways sometimes have to negotiate tortuous accesses from the street to get on to the correct station platform. In the city centre, conventional railways either stop short of offices and shops or decant their passengers deep underground in the bowels of the city. Some of the walks through passages and up and down stairs on the London Underground seem as long as the station spacings themselves, and that is before you start your onward walk on the surface to wherever you're going.

THE GOLDFISH BOWL EFFECT

The modern tram's large windows and in-street operation make it easy for passers-by and police patrols to see what's happening on board. This security is a two-way affair; well-used trams mean lots of pairs of passengers' eyes looking outwards and observing what is going on in the street. A clear view right through the interior of a light rail vehicle adds to passengers' feeling of confidence, as does the driver's ability to look round and see into the passenger area as well as forward into the street scene.

A WINNING COMBINATION

In a nutshell, then, thanks to its unrivalled alignment flexibility the modern tram compounds the speed of the train with the accessiblity of the bus and adds cleanliness, ambience and high marks on the ecological front for good measure. Light rail also has a supreme ability to cater for the needs of people with a personal mobility problem. However the delivery of these benefits requires the highest standards of professional skill, political altruism and public forbearance.

The local conventional train, then, is comfortable and fast if you take the trouble to find it and are prepared to knuckle under to its idiosyncracies. It is generally the best solution for inter-urban journeys. The bus will take you near to your home and destination but is slower and less comfortable than the train. The train can shift many more passengers per hour than the bus, if it can attract and retain them. New railways take years and plenty of money to justify and construct but a new bus route can be introduced or abandoned overnight, as hapless passengers have discovered since deregulation. Light rail fills the gap.

European Developments

Above: A tram in the busy shopping street of Leidsestraat in Amsterdam. This street is very narrow and has interlaced track. Trams enter and leave the interlaced section without any signalling. *Peter Fox*

Many people are apt to wonder why South Yorkshire has chosen a tram system rather than other cheaper modes of transport like trolley buses or just improved bus services. To understand this, a look at developments in Europe is appropriate.

Attitudes to trams varied between different countries in Europe. In Switzerland, Austria, Germany, Belgium and the Netherlands, trams have generally been retained, whereas in Great Britain, only Blackpool continued running its tram system. In France most cities got rid of their trams, but Lille, St. Etienne and Marseille retained them.

Some of the reasons why trams have been successful in many European countries are as follows:

- Measures were taken to ensure that the trams had their own rights of way so that they had an advantage in journey time over their competitors.
- Modern off-vehicle ticketing systems meant that large articulated vehicles could be used, without the employment of extra staff and without delays due to passengers paying the driver when boarding.
- These roomy modern vehicles could give a higher degree of passenger comfort than could a bus.
- The modern trams gave passengers a comfortable quiet ride due to such features as modern bogie design and resilient wheels (steel wheels with rubber inserts between the wheel centre and the steel tyre).

AMSTERDAM, NETHERLANDS

Amsterdam's trams are almost as famous as its canals and its red-light district. The sleek-looking articulated yellow-painted trams are the main form of public transport in the capital city of the Netherlands. At one time their future was in doubt, but since the system was modernised in the 70s, it has been realised that Amsterdam could not really cope without them, as its road system would have been completely overwhelmed with cars. The trams are used by all classes of people, as is the case in most cities which have an efficient public transport system and unlike in many British cities where the policies of successive governments have ensured that public transport is only used if one has not got a car available.

ZÜRICH, SWITZERLAND

Another city where the tram is the main form of public transport is Zürich, Switzerland's major financial centre - a very affluent city where most commuters prefer to leave their cars at home and travel to their banks and offices by tram.

UTRECHT - EUROPE'S FIRST NEW TRAMWAY

The city of Utrecht in the Netherlands was the first city in Europe to reverse the trend and set up a new light rail system to connect the city centre with two new suburbs at Nieuwegein and IJsselstein. This system which opened in 1981 was a fully reserved-track system and was operated by the Netherland Railways (NS), but is now operated by the Midnet bus company. Its success was to lead France to consider building new tram systems in a number of cities.

NANTES, FRANCE

The oil crisis of the 70s led to the French government taking the initiative of recommending medium-sized cities to investigate the possibility of reintroducing tramways. The state would pay 50% of the infrastructure cost. Nantes decided to take the lead in this, the result being line one which opened between Haluchère and Commerce on 7th January 1985 and between Bellevue and Commerce on 18th February 1985. The rest of the cost of this line was met by the versement transport, a local payroll tax which can be

Right: A Nantes tram passes the Château des Ducs de Bretagne. *Peter Fox*

Above: The Nantes trams serve the main railway station. *Peter Fox*

levied by conurbations with a population greater than 300,000. Companies with ten or more employees have to pay this tax, which in Nantes was set at 1.5%.

Unlike the Utrecht system, the Nantes system is a true tramway, with most of the track running alongside main roads. Parts of the route are similar to former tramways, and there is also a part of the first section which runs alongside an SNCF (French Railways) freight line. Such was the success of this, France's first new tramway, that the layout was soon extended to a new interchange and park-and-ride facility at La Beaujoire, and a new north-south line has recently been finished to complement the first east-west route. The two-section trams have had to be extended to three sections to accommodate the increase in passenger volumes and the new centre sections have low floors to accommodate mobility-impaired passengers following on from the Grenoble experience described below.

GRENOBLE, FRANCE

The second new French tramway to be built was at Grenoble. This opened in February 1987 and differed from Nantes in two ways. Firstly, it featured true street-running in the City Centre, including some pedestrianised areas. Secondly, a new type of tram was designed. It was originally intended that the Grenoble trams would match the so-called French standard tram built for the Nantes system, but as a result of public consultation, a low-floor vehicle was designed which with 245 mm platforms at each stop would permit almost level access into the car. Two doors were fitted with a small retractable ramp to bridge the gap between platform and car, so that there would be easy access for wheelchairs. Thus disabled people would be able to use a regular public transport service for the first time, and the facilities would also make travelling easier for others. About 60 wheelchair passengers each day now use the tram; a recent survey produced such comments as "the tramway is an extraordinary source of freedom", and "the tramway makes a significant contribution to my integration into city life".

Grenoble tramway line A has been in public service since September 1987. 12 million passengers were carried in the first year, some 26% more than the equivalent bus routes replaced by the tramway. By 1989 18 of the initial fleet of 20 trams were in peak service, with a car every four minutes on the 8.8 km route. Introduction of the tramway permitted 72 buses to be withdrawn from parallel routes; there remain 25 motor and trolleybus routes served by some 200 vehicles, but the trams now carry 30% of the total system patronage, or about 65 000 passengers each day. About 12% of these passengers were not previously public transport users, and 5% of passengers have been identified as former motorists. This has resulted in 2000 fewer private car journeys per day. Since then, many more motorists have turned to the tram, another route has been built to the University and further extensions are planned.

Below: The tramway system in Grenoble has been very successful and pioneered the idea of low-floor trams. It has been a model for many systems including, to a certain extent, the Sheffield system. This photograph is taken in Rue Félix-Poulat which used to be a main highway. Trams and pedestrians now co-exist happily in this street. *Peter Fox*

STRASBOURG, FRANCE

The new tramway in Strasbourg, home of the European parliament was to have had trams built by an Italian firm, Socimi. These trams were to be of a revolutionary design featuring a low-floor throughout with a futuristic appearance. Socimi went into liquidation, however, and the company which was to supply the electrical equipment, ABB elected to also produce the vehicle to the original concept. This company now owns the former British Railways workshops at Derby, York and Crewe and the trams have been manufactured at York.

Left: The futuristic ABB Eurotrams in Strasbourg were built in York. At the time the South Yorkshire Supertrams were ordered there were no companies in the UK building trams. *David Haydock*

Above: A pair of Karlsruhe trams in the traffic-calmed centre of the village of Linkenheim. *Peter Fox*

KARLSRUHE, GERMANY

An interesting development in Karlsruhe, Germany is a tram which can not only operate along the street and along purpose-built reservations, but can also run on the German Railways' main lines. The trams have to work at the normal d.c. voltage as well as at the standard high voltage a.c. used on the main line. They have proved so popular that German Railways have bought some themselves and some are to be fitted with toilets for use during excursions to Switzerland! These trams are built by Siemens, the same manufacturer as the South Yorkshire Supertrams. Thus we can now see the ultimate in flexibility!

Other trams in Karlsruhe feature panoramic centre cars for trips to the Black Forest. These cars have 2 + 1 seating in a vehicle which has the same width as the Sheffield ones and have tables for the service of refreshments!

Below: Certain Karlsruhe trams have centre sections with panoramic windows and tables for working into the Black Forest. *Peter Fox*

New Tramways in Britain

New tramways and light rail systems are being built or planned in many British cities. The first light rail schemes to be built were fully segregated schemes with no street running. These were the Tyne & Wear Metro in the Newcastle area and the Docklands Light Railway in London. Although classed as light rail because of their characteristics (vehicle design, track alignments and gradients), these systems are not tramways because the vehicles cannot operate on-street.

MANCHESTER METROLINK

The traditional British street tramway never died out, as the Blackpool and Fleetwood Tramway is still in operation, and whilst much of this is on reserved track, some is still on the street, particularly in Fleetwood. The first of the second generation of British tramways is the Manchester Metrolink system. The first phase of this system consists of two existing railway lines, the Manchester-Altrincham and Manchester-Bury which have been linked together with a new section of street tramway through Manchester City Centre, together with a link to Manchester Piccadilly station. Since most of the stations on the route are existing BR stations, the system has been designed with high platforms and the trams have high floors. There are only four new stations which are in the City Centre. One of these, Piccadilly Gardens, has high platforms and the other three have a strange "profiled platform" arrangement whereby that part of the platform opposite the centre pair of the tram doors is at floor level, but the rest is at a lower level. It has to be said that these stations are nowhere near as neat as the low-platform ones in Sheffield. The Manchester Metrolink system has been very successful and has succeeded in attracting a large number of car users onto public transport. An ambitious programme of extensions is planned.

CROYDON TRAMLINK

The Croydon Tramlink scheme will re-introduce trams to London for the first time since 1952. The route runs from Wimbledon to Croydon Centre and thence to Beckenham, Elmers End and New Addington. Starting at Wimbledon the service replaces the current BR Wimbledon-West Croydon service, running on-street on a one-way system through Croydon Town Centre. To the east of Croydon centre the route is a mixture of new segregated alignment, disused railway alignments and running alongside existing railways to reach New Addington and Beckenham Junction. The project has received an Act of Parliament and funding has been promised by the Secretary of State for Transport.

MIDLAND METRO

Midland Metro line 1 is a 20 km light rail line intended to contribute to the regeneration of the 'Black Country' (so called because the soil is black unlike the red soil of neighbouring Birmingham). This is an area of declining traditional industry. The scheme consists of the re-opening of the former GWR line from Birmingham Snow Hill to Wolverhampton as far as Monmore Green on the outskirts of Wolverhampton Town Centre from where the line runs on-street to Market Street.

Above: A Manchester tram in Aytoun Street near Piccadilly Gardens *Peter Fox*

The scheme has been promoted by Centro (West Midlands PTE) with support from the West Midlands Metropolitan districts as part of a 'package' bid covering all forms of transport. It received an Act of Parliament as far back as November 1989 but has been held up for lack of Government finance. The Government has recently announced funding for the project but this is conditional on "a significant proportion of its total cost being found locally". What this means is not explained. Despite the Government press release stating that the scheme had got the "Green light", we understand that only £5 million has been released for spending in the 1995-6 financial year.

OTHER SCHEMES

Many other cities have tram schemes in the pipeline, the most advanced being Nottingham, Leeds, South Hampshire and Glasgow.

Below: A Manchester tram entering the "undercroft" underneath Manchester Piccadilly station. *Peter Fox*

The Supertram Project

THE ADVENT OF SUPERTRAM

Between 1972 and 1976, the Sheffield & Rotherham Land Use Transportation Study (SRLUTS) considered the anticipated passenger movement requirements upto and including the 1990s. An increased demand for commuting into the city centre and the growth in service industries was envisaged. Many different options to meet the future transport needs of the area were examined, and one of these was for an extensive network of modern tramways. The final report of this study recommended amongst other things "that routes to Rotherham, Shiregreen, Middlewood, Stannington, Totley, Jordanthorpe, and Mosborough be safeguarded to allow eventual construction of a segregated public transport system. This could be improved buses, modern tramways or a new technology, if appropriate". Coinciding with the SRLUTS, in 1974 local Government was re-organised and this brought into existence from 1st April the South Yorkshire Passenger Transport Executive. The PTE took over the old Corporation bus fleets of Sheffield, Rotherham and Doncaster and merged them into a new fleet. The PTE could also assume responsibity for local rail services. The PTE development plan which was published in 1978 concluded that "electric traction is the most likely future alternative for all longer term transit systems in the country", and approved the SRLUTS findings regarding the "Segregated Passenger Transport System" (SPTS). A similar approval was given by the County Structure Plan in 1979.

In 1982, the SPTS team reviewed in great detail the options available for improvement of public transport in Sheffield, including bus based systems such as trolleybus and guided busways, and also rail based systems: totally segregated (i.e. elevated, ground level and in tunnel) before the recommendation was made to South Yorkshire County Council in 1983, that a modern tramway system was the preferred option. It is interesting to see why this mode was the preference. Basically the study showed that, "if segregation could be justified, giving reduced running times and increased reliability, with attendant benefits to both passenger and operator, the light rail system was the most cost effective. Trolleybus associated infrastructure costs, could not produce the productivity sufficient to finance the investment, because of the limitation on the vehicle size".

In the meantime the corridors to Hillsborough in the north west of the city, and Mosborough in the south east via the City Centre, a distance of about 25 km had been selected for detailed assessment to ascertain the most cost effective mode. This, as has been seen, was a light rail system which has become known as "Supertram" and a Private Bill entitled "The South Yorkshire Light Rail Transit Bill" was presented to Parliament in November 1985.

THE ABORTIVE 'MINITRAM' PROPOSAL

One proposal considered in the Land Use Transportation study was known as 'Minitram'. The name was a misnomer, as the vehicles were not trams at all because they could not run in he street. They were small driverless electric vehicles which ran on a special guideway, generally overhead. Stations would have been a complicated affair with lifts and escalators as well as stairs. An article in the 'New Scientist' descibed the scheme as 'an ugly white elephant' and a 'costly fraud', as a similar scheme in the USA was at that time suffering a cost overrun of 800%. The whole idea was abandoned after being thrown out by the Sheffield public as environmentally obtrusive and the study team did not consider it value for money.

Artist's impression of how Castle Square would look. Note that the overhead structure casts no shadow, even though it is a sunny day.

PARLIAMENTARY POWERS

The first Bill was deposited in Parliament on the 19th November 1985, The preamble shows it to "empower the South Yorkshire Passenger Transport Executive to develop and operate a system of light rail transit; to authorise the construction of works and the acquisition of land for that purpose; to confer further powers upon the Executive; and for other purposes". The works to be authorised were to start by Winn Gardens at Middlewood to travel by way of Middlewood Road, Langsett Road, with a junction at Hillsborough Corner with a branch from Holme Lane and Stannington, then Infirmary Road, Netherthorpe Road, Glossop Road, West Street through the City Centre, the Railway Station up through Norfolk Park Estate, Manor, Gleadless to Birley and Halfway, with a further spur to Herdings from Gleadless Townend. Before the Bill had reached the Opposed Bills Committee in the House of Commons, the PTE agreed to withdraw the line from Malin Bridge to Stannington at the request of the City Council.

There were two official objectors, a residents' group and National Car Parks Ltd. and due to elements of doubt as to how committed Sheffield City Council was, the procedure was adjourned on two occasions, before passing the Commons stage on the 20th April 1988. The House of Lords Opposed Committee also heard objections from a group of residents and traders together with the City of Sheffield & District Chamber of Trade, during July 1988. The bill received Royal Assent on 27th October 1988. So after a period of nearly three years the way was open for further advancement of the scheme.

Supertram is partly funded by a grant from the European Development Fund.

Whilst the 1985 Bill was plodding its way through the many intricacies of the two Houses of Parliament, two major pieces of legislation had occurred which had led to questions being asked about the Supertram proposals. Firstly in April 1986 South Yorkshire County Council was abolished and Sheffield City Council became responsible for highway matters for all non-trunk roads in the District. Secondly in October 1986 all bus operation in Great Britain outside London was deregulated, which led to SYPTE losing its powers to direct all bus operation in the area. Deregulation of course, then posed the problem of how Supertram would fit in to an uncoordinated deregulated system. The original intention was for an integrated system which would have maximised revenue and minimised costs for public transport services in the city, but this had been lost by the Government's actions. In 1987, the viability of Supertram was therefore examined yet again and the study concluded that there was still an economic case for Supertram.

In order for the City Council to reassess the proposals and give their unreserved backing to the Bill, then stalled in The Commons, a period of intensive Consultation with an exhibition housed in a plywood mock up of a Supertram on the Cathedral forecourt took place between 12th to 26th September 1987. Public attitude responses were very encouraging with 65% of those questioned at the exhibition stating that the scheme should go ahead, and a slightly higher 67% of those interviewed in their own homes recording the same advice. Public meetings were arranged at various centres affected by the proposals, and as expected attracted a fairly low turnout. It must be noted that the majority of the comments made at these meetings, were negative, but on analysing the returns it was obvious that this was mainly due to lack of knowledge of the proposals. Suffice to say here that armed with these figures and the Re-assessment Study outlined above, the City Council at its meeting in October 1987 overwhelmingly endorsed the scheme and thereby released the Bill in Parliament.

A Second Line

The City Council's support for the line from Middlewood to Mosborough came with certain conditions attached, namely that a new routing had to be found from Manor Top along City Road to Park Grange Road, due to a council policy of renovating certain parts of the Manor Estate, and that the Passenger Transport Executive promote a further Bill to Parliament extending the system through the Lower Don Valley. The aim of the latter was the regeneration of this former industrial heartland of the city now mostly derelict after the collapse of the city's world famous steel industry. Another aim was to serve the new sports stadia being built for the 1991 World Student Games. Two further requirements were that if a second Bill was passed by Parliament, the depot should be re-sited in the Lower Don Valley away from the original site at Halfway, and finally that construction of the tramway be re-phased so that the line to Meadowhall be opened first (originally to serve the Games).

In February 1988 therefore the South Yorkshire Passenger Authority authorised the PTE to undertake a study to evaluate a route for this second line, which had to connect with the original one to form a network and be capable of subsequent extension to nearby Rotherham and any future Sheffield Airport then being seriously considered in the Lower Don Valley. This study had to be completed by July 1988.

A bill was presented in 1988 and the works detailed in the Bill were for the formation of a delta junction at Park Square with lines from Commercial Street and South Street i.e. of the original line, to meet the new line from the north east of the city. Line 2 was authorised to go via the Parkway Viaduct along the south side of the Sheffield Parkway, over the Midland railway line, across Bernard Road at grade and alongside a widened Cricket Inn Road in cutting. The line to then cross over the Sheffield Parkway and run beside the new depot site at Nunnery. Continuing northeastwards over the ex Great Central railway at Woodbourn Road to Staniforth Road then over the Sheffield & South Yorkshire Canal and to join the railway alignment to Tinsley. Here the line to turn westwards to run along the course of the former railway to Smithywood (and previously Barnsley) crossing over the River Don and terminating alongside the Midland railway at Meadowhall. The latter section brought the line into Rotherham for a few short metres.

The whole of the route is segregated, with crossings at Bernard Road, Aston Street, Woodbourn Road, Staniforth Road, Shirland Lane and Alsing Road. Various road widenings were incorporated in the Bill, as was the provision of a new footbridge over the Sheffield & South Yorkshire Canal, to the north of the tram bridge.

Above: On 23rd May 1994, The system was officially opened by HRH the Princess Royal. Chief Executive of South Yorkshire Light Rail Transit, John Davis is explaining something to her. *Richard Bolsover*

This unopposed Bill received support from many quarters, including that of the Chamber of Trade, who it will be remembered objected to the initial route through the city centre. It was of course fulfilling parts of the City Council's requirements outlined earlier. However a most unusual delay was encountered just as it was expected to receive a final reading. A furious row concerning other items in Parliament, nothing whatsoever to do with Supertram held up Parliamentary procedures and threatened to delay Royal Assent. Fortunately common sense returned and the Bill passed the final hurdle and received Assent on 21st December 1989.

A wholly owned subsidiary of the PTE, South Yorkshire Supertram Ltd (SYSL1, now 'South Yorkshire Light Rail Ltd.') was established in 1989 to carry the project forward. Later, another company, known as SYSL2 (now 'South Yorkshire Supertram Ltd.') was formed whose only asset is the concession to operate the system. At a later date the Conservative Government requires that this company be privatised. The infrastructure and vehicles will however remain publicly owned.

FUNDING THE SCHEME

It was decided to apply to the Government for a grant under Section 56 of the Transport act 1968. Almost inevitably whilst discussions were in force the criteria for the payment of this type of grant were radically altered and further work had to be instigated. The new rules meant that approval of new rail infrastructure depended on the scheme being profitable, on it being the most cost effective way of meeting defined social needs, on developers being prepared to make contributions, on the cost being less than the discounted sum of the revenues to be earned from passengers and on benefits the system will produce for non-users.

Public transport investment, which includes the Supertram scheme, was therefore justified on the basis of the benefits it would bring to those who would not use the facilities, in such ways as alleviating traffic congestion etc, and not on the benefits to the users. The latter were expected to pay for their own benefits through higher fares.

Against this background of "moving goalposts", application was made by the PTE to the Department of Transport for grant towards the cost of the scheme in late 1988, initially for Line 1 but later to include the Meadowhall line as well.

November 1989, brought a further set back in the building of the Meadowhall line to serve the sites for the World Student Games to be held in the city in July 1991, in that the Government told the local authorities resources would not be available in 1990/1 for the scheme. It was stated that central government were already investing many millions of pounds in transport infrastructure referring in great detail to the "Road Programme" as though that in isolation would bring benefits to all, totally ignoring how the traffic generated by such building would be catered for in urban areas. Private investors had already shown willingness to get involved in the scheme, which was one of the demands of the Government in their Section 56 guidelines. It is interesting to see that the Sheffield Development Corporation secured a further £14 million grant, at this time, to ensure the building of a highway through the Lower Don Valley. Urgent meetings with Whitehall officials in an attempt to keep the project alive and the team together met with a similar refusal of grant in February 1990. Although it was accepted that the project should be safeguarded and an allocation of £3.5 million for this purpose and that of taking the programme forward.

However the best possible news for the Supertram scheme and Sheffield/South Yorkshire in general was delivered by Mr Roger Freeman, the Minister for Public Transport, on 11th December 1990 when he announced that resources had been made available to fund the majority of the project costs which were expected to total £240 million. Contributions were also announced as coming from Meadowhall Centre, the Sheffield Development Corporation and Sheffield City Council. It was however stated that the Government required the operation to be transferred to the private sector in due course. Mr Freeman in announcing that the project was the largest local scheme to be approved outside London for nearly twenty years, also assured everyone that local poll-tax payers would not be paying for the new transport system. Unfortunately a political arguement over possible council charge-capping brought further delay, until being resolved in April 1991.

Jack Meridith, Chairman of South Yorkshire Passenger Transport Authority with the Master and Mistress Cutler, Mr. and Mrs.Christopher Jewitt on the occasion of the official opening of the tram route to the Cathedral on 20th February 1995. Also present on this occasion was the Bishop of Sheffield, the Right Revd. David Lunn *Peter Fox*

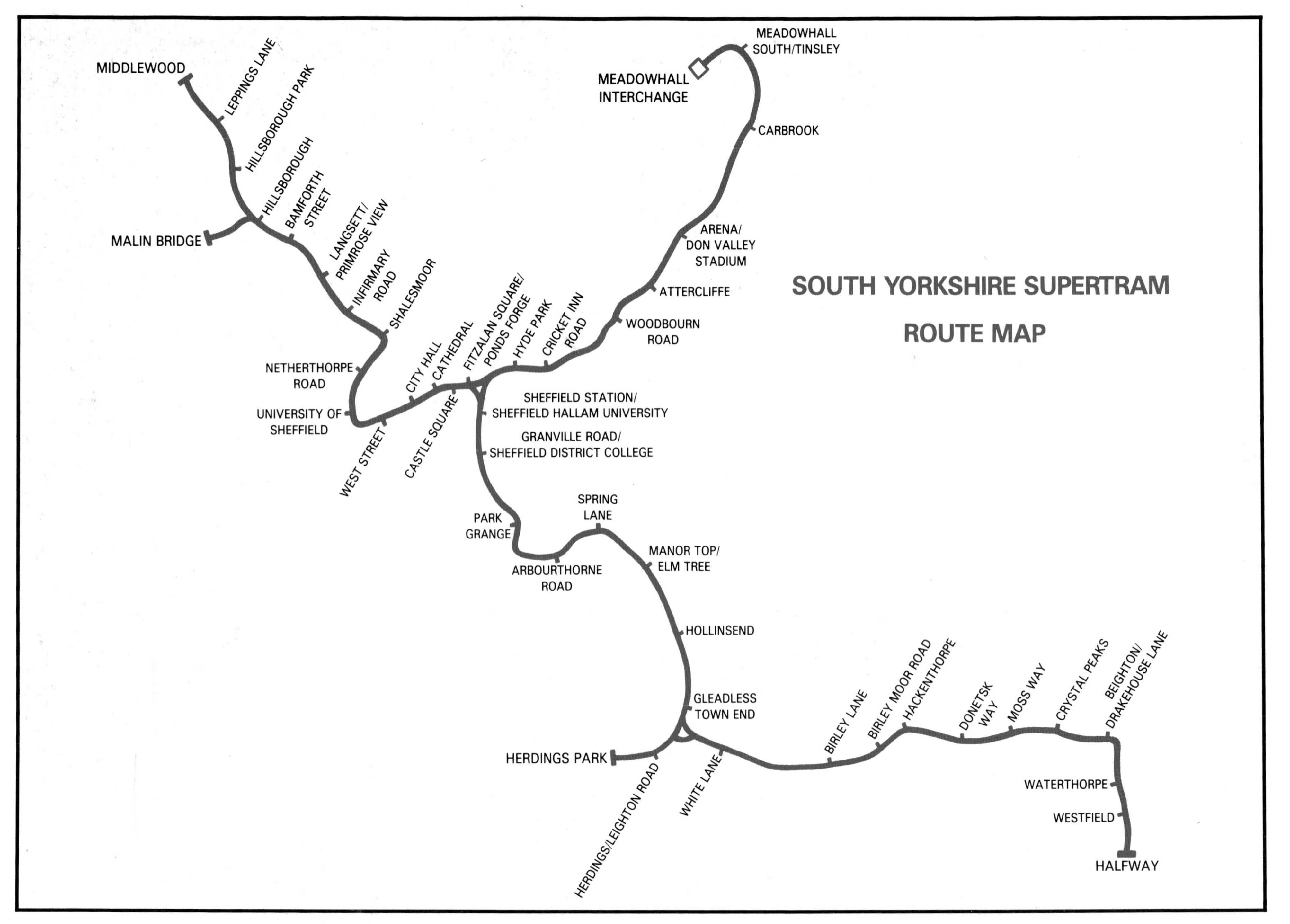
SOUTH YORKSHIRE SUPERTRAM
ROUTE MAP
MIDDLEWOOD
LEPPINGS LANE
HILLSBOROUGH PARK
HILLSBOROUGH
MALIN BRIDGE
BAMFORTH STREET
LANGSETT/ PRIMROSE VIEW
INFIRMARY ROAD
SHALESMOOR
NETHERTHORPE ROAD
UNIVERSITY OF SHEFFIELD
WEST STREET
CITY HALL
CATHEDRAL
CASTLE SQUARE
FITZALAN SQUARE/ PONDS FORGE
HYDE PARK
CRICKET INN ROAD
WOODBOURN ROAD
ATTERCLIFFE
ARENA/ DON VALLEY STADIUM
CARBROOK
MEADOWHALL SOUTH/TINSLEY
MEADOWHALL INTERCHANGE
SHEFFIELD STATION/ SHEFFIELD HALLAM UNIVERSITY
GRANVILLE ROAD/ SHEFFIELD DISTRICT COLLEGE
PARK GRANGE
ARBOURTHORNE ROAD
SPRING LANE
MANOR TOP/ ELM TREE
HOLLINSEND
GLEADLESS TOWN END
HERDINGS PARK
HERDINGS/LEIGHTON ROAD
WHITE LANE
BIRLEY LANE
BIRLEY MOOR ROAD
HACKENTHORPE
DONETSK WAY
MOSS WAY
CRYSTAL PEAKS
BEIGHTON/ DRAKEHOUSE LANE
WATERTHORPE
WESTFIELD
HALFWAY

A PIONEERING SYSTEM

Right: Supertram is the first system to have ballasted partially-segregated track running alongside the street as shown by this view taken on Woodbourn Road. The 'wavy wall' was paid for by a Government grant to Sheffield City Council for use on environmental enhancements to the scheme. *Peter Fox*

Unlike the Manchester Metrolink system which is basically a linking together of two ex-BR inter-urban railway routes by a section of tramway in the City Centre, the South Yorkshire Supertram scheme is an urban system. Thus it has more frequent stops and is designed with low-platform access. The system has a number of features which at present make it unique in British cities.

It is the first new system to feature mixed running of light rail vehicles and ordinary traffic. This, of course is what used to happen with the old street tramways, but there are important differences. Firstly traffic management measures are being undertaken to ensure that most of the streets in which problems could occur have their through car traffic diverted onto other streets and that the tramway is allowed a through path by providing loading/parking and bus bays outside the swept path alignment. Secondly, passengers will board at proper platforms offering level access.

It is the first new system to have ballasted partially-segregated track running alongside the street. This is a cost-effective method of construction and at the same time it is immediately apparent that it should not be used as a walkway.

It is the first system to be built with low platforms. These fit in with well with the streetscape and present a much neater apperance than the high platforms or profiled platforms that have been built in Central Manchester.

It is the first system to have long three-section articulated vehicles. The decision to adopt such vehicles rather than shorter two-section vehicles which are equipped for multiple operation as in Manchester and in the proposed Leeds system means shorter less obtrusive platforms.

It is the first system to feature tactile markings on platforms to assist blind and partially-sighted passengers.

Below: Street running on City Road. This main road features shared running with general traffic. Unfortunately it was not possible to provide a separate route for the light rail system in this case. *Paul Jackson*

CONSTRUCTION

On 26th September 1990 after an extremely exhaustive tendering process, it was announced by South Yorkshire Supertram Ltd that Balfour Beatty Power Construction Ltd had been selected to design and build the infrastructure and that Siemens/Duewag would supply the 25 double articulated Light Rail Vehicles Highway design including certain structures was however carried out by Design & Building Services (DBS) a subsidiary of Sheffield City council. The contract with Balfour Beatty involves work on trackwork, power supply, overhead conductor system, the depot construction and equipment, and signalling. Other contracts dealing with Operation and Maintenance were not dealt with at that time. Subsequently Balfour Beatty and Siemens Transportation Systems Ltd received contracts to provide core maintenance services, the responsibilities being split according to their respective areas of expertise. Operation is being carried out by a company specially set up for the purpose -South Yorkshire Supertram Operating Company Ltd. (SYSOC). Operation and maintenance is based at Nunnery Depot.

The building of the system is being carried out in the following sequence:

Phase 1 Meadowhall to Commercial Street, and Interchange;

Phase 2 Interchange to Spring Lane (City Road);

Phase 5 Spring Lane to Gleadless Townend and Herdings;

Phase 6 Gleadless Townend to Donetsk Way;

Phase 7 Donetsk Way to Halfway;

Phase 3 Commercial Street to Cathedral;
Phase 4 Cathedral to Shalesmoor;

Above: Construction underway on the bridge over the Sheffield Canal near Staniforth Road. In the background can be seen the new Technology Park. *Peter Fox*

Phase 8 Shalesmoor to Middlewood/Malin Bridge.

Actual opening dates to the public so far are:

21st March 1994: Fitzalan Square to Meadowhall

22nd August 1994: Fitzalan Square to Spring Lane

05th December 1994: Spring Lane to Gleadless Townend

18th February 1995: Fitzalan Square to Cathedral

27th February 1995: Cathedral to Shalesmoor

Construction of the infrastructure commenced on 5th August 1991 on Phase 1, i.e. City Centre to Meadowhall. Mr Roger Freeman, returned to the city on 16th September 1991, to officially commemorate the commencement of the construction work, in a ceremony at Park Square.

On the railway alignment and on segregated stretches, the work on the actual tramway has been relatively straight forward, without the need for road closures except for work on the street crossings. On the roads where the tram will run with other traffic it has led to road closures, diversions etc, which obviously are regrettable but necessary. The benefits the scheme will bring to the city will surely far outweigh the temporary inconvenience that has been caused.

The work involves the construction of two large viaducts, one underpass and around thirty other structures, mainly bridges, retaining walls and culverts. An estimated 1750 tonnes of steel, 4000 tonnes of reinforcement steelwork and a staggering 23000 cubic metres of concrete are being used. Approximately 60 km of trackbed are being laid together with 120 km of rail. Over 50% of the rail is grooved tram rail inserted into channels in the trackbed and encapsulated in a resin known as Edilon Corkelast VO. The overhead power supply will consist of approximately 120 km of contact wire supported at a height of 5-6 metres by some 2300 supports, poles or building fixtures. Transmitton Ltd (a division of Balfour Beatty) has provided a PC based "Supervisory Control & Data Acquisition" system (SCADA), based at Nunnery depot, to control the power supply to the 750 V d.c. overhead wire.

Left: The Parkway Viaduct under construction as seen from the Canal Basinon 17th May 1992. The Canal Basin is now being redeveloped. *Peter Fox*

THE HALFWAY/HERDINGS ROUTE

Leaving Cathedral we follow one of Sheffield's former main tramway routes through the City Centre. High Street is altered so that a single bus lane runs uphill to the south of the tramway. At Castle Square the former 'hole in the road' has been filled in and in its place a newly-pedestrianised area with a tram stop has been substituted. The next stop is in Commercial Street (known as Fitzalan Square/Ponds Forge), This street was a dual carriageway leading onto an enormous round traffic island called 'Park Square'. This is probably the most important road junction in Sheffield, as it is the end of the Sheffield Parkway, the main route into Sheffield from the M1 motorway. Clearly the route has to be segregated at this point, and the solution has been to use the former eastbound lane of Commercial Street as the tramway. At the bottom, a 70 metre span bowstring arch bridge leads to the island where the line turns sharp right over a single-span concrete bridge to run along Granville Street at an upper level parallel to the Midland station. A station has been built here and will be connected both to the new Transport Interchange (bus station) and to the Midland Railway station.

Above: Tram 07 in the snow on Park Grange Road on 28th January 1995. The tram is on an inbound working near St. Aidan's Road. *Paul Jackson*

The line crosses Shrewsbury Road and Granville Road on the level and the stop here is a staggered one with the inbound platform between these two roads and the outbound one to the south of Granville Road. Past Granville, the line starts to climb, helped by the Norfolk Park Road Viaduct, needed because the ruling 10% gradient would be exceeded without it. At the end of the viaduct the track runs on reservation at the south side of the road and there is provision for a stop here although one has not actually been built. The track from here is on-street, shared with general traffic. The gradient along the viaduct is 1 in 20, but the climb up Park Grange Road on the Norfolk Park Estate soon gets steeper so that around 400 metres of the route are at 1 in 12. Park Grange Road curves to the east and levels out and just past Spring Lane, the route turns right to run up City Road to Elm Tree. This section formed part of the old Intake tram route. Originally, the new tramway was to have run through the Manor Estate, when it was thought that the area was to be redeveloped, but there was a change of plan by the City Council. This meant that the opportunity of a new reserved track route was lost, and since the existing road layout was unsuitable, the decision was taken to run up City Road.

At Manor Top (Elm Tree), the route turns right along the outer ring road, Ridgeway Road. The alignment was to have been along the central reservation of the dual carriageway but there was not enough room without demolishing most of the trees along the side of the road. Thus the alignment used is in the outer lanes of the road, but with a separate reserved track route inbound between Hollinsend Road and Manor Top. The Manor Top stop is on reservation at the sides of the road and the inbound tracks have to cross the traffic lanes by means of a signalised crossing. The Hollinsend and Gleadless Townend stops are in the centre of the dual carriageway on a short reserved section and is accessed by pedestrian crossings.

Below: Tram 18 leaves Manor Top and crosses Hurlfield Road on an outbound working to Gleadless Townend. *Paul Jackson*

At Gleadless Townend, the main line turns east down White Lane, whilst the Herdings branch carries straight on for a short distance along the road, eventually bearing west and leaving the road alignment to run through open space and a recent plantation for around 600 m to a terminus at Raeburn Road. The highest point of the system is on this section at 212.09 m (694 ft) above sea level, having climbed 143.65 m (471 ft) from the city centre. There are two stops on this spur, Herdings, just behind the 'Cutlers Arms' pub and Herdings park at the terminus.

The alignment along White Lane is on-street until the 'Old Harrow' public house is reached. Just past here is the county boundary. On entering Derbyshire, the line runs through fields for around 900 m on ballasted track eventually running back into Sheffield on Birley Lane, although the inbound track is soon on its own reservation again. Birley Moor Road is crossed and the line then starts to descend into an area which has been recently developed as a satellite township to Sheffield known collectively as Mosborough. The alignment from here onwards is virtually all on reservation, either alongside the roads or across fields.

The new shopping and leisure complex known as 'Crystal Peaks' has its own bus station, and the tram station will be adjacent to this. The terminus at Halfway is 69.67 m (228 ft) above sea level.

THE MIDDLEWOOD/MALIN BRIDGE ROUTE

Left: Netherthorpe Road is the only island platform on the system. A tram is seen on an inbound driver-training run on 25th February 1995. *Peter Fox*

Our journey starts in Cathedral Square in Church Street. On the right is Sheffield Cathedral (Anglican) on the left is the Cutlers' Hall. We are still on the former Crookes/Walkley tram route as we pass through West Street and Glossop Road, but the former Middlewood and Malin Bridge routes turned off at what is now called Castle Square to run down Angel Street.

The old tram route to Crookes ran up Hounsfield Road, not now a through road. We turn sharp right onto the Inner Ring Road where a stop serves the University. An underpass takes the line under the Brook Hill roundabout and the line then runs in the centre of the Netherthorpe Road dual carriageway. The stop on Netherthorpe Road is unusual, as it is an island platform. The line continues into Hoyle Street and curves off to the left to run along Shalesmoor and Langsett Road. Alignment on this section is entirely in the carriageway. It should be noted that the parallel Penistone Road has been converted to a dual carriageway, this being another recommendation of the 1970s SRLUTS study, so that most of the Supertram route will become public transport and access only. We pass the former Hillsborough Barracks on the right, for many years used by the "Burdall's Gravy Salt" company, but now a shopping precinct.

The short Malin Bridge branch turns off to the left at Hillsborough Corner, where there is a prosperous suburban shopping area. The building of this branch necessitated the demolition of a narrow block of shops adjacent to the River Don. This branch is entirely on-street. On the right we pass the "Tramways Medical Centre", built on the site of the former Malin Bridge tram depot. The line terminates before Malin Bridge itself adjacent to a large number of residential streets. Malin Bridge is the gateway to the beautiful Rivelin Valley.

After passing Sheffield Wednesday's Hillsborough football ground on the right, the main line carries on along Middlewood Road to the Middlewood terminus, which is to the right of the carriageway. The old Middlewood and Malin Bridge tram routes are followed all the way from Shalesmoor.

Below: A crew-training tram at the West Street stop, just outside Blackwell's bookshop. The majority of span wires are affixed to the buildings in this area. *Peter Fox*

THE MEADOWHALL LINE

The route to Meadowhall diverges from the Halfway/Hwerdings route at a triangular junction on the Park Square roundabout and bears left on a six-span post-tensioned reinforced concrete segmental viaduct which is 350 m long. Unlike the Mosborough and Middlewood routes, this line has no street-running, although there are a number of street crossings. The viaduct runs along the south side of the Sheffield Parkway and after leaving this we cross the BR Midland main line on a steel girder bridge. After crossing Bernard Road by means of a crossing signalled by traffic lights, we arrive at the Hyde Park stop. The adjacent Hyde park flats have been refurbished, whilst others have been demolished. The line now follows the route of the former road known as Aston Street to the Cricket Inn Road stop. This is served by a special park and ride car park where motorists can leave their cars and travel by tram to the City Centre or University for £2. The line then swings north to cross the Sheffield Parkway road and then turns east with the line to the depot leaving on the left. This depot is built partially on the site of the former London & North Western Railway engine shed and partly on the site of the former Nunnery Colliery Exchange Sidings (not on the site of Nunnery Carriage Sidings as erroneously stated elsewhere). The line then swings around to the north and another spur from the depot trails in on the left. We cross the ex-Great Central Railway line from Sheffield to Worksop and then run along Woodbourn Road on reservation, in an area which has seen most of its old industry and all its slum housing demolished. The road is on our right as far as Worthing Road/Stadium Way where we cross over so that the road is on our left. On the right is the retaining wall of of Woodbourn stadium which has been decorated in an unusual wavy pattern, this decoration being financed by Government money made available to Sheffield City Council for environmental enhancements associated with the Supertram project. There is a stop adjacent to this wall.

At the end of Woodbourn Road, the track crosses Staniforth Road and then an interesting bridge takes the route over the Sheffield Canal. The design of this bridge takes as its inspiration the bridge over the Ironbridge Gorge in Shropshire (the world's first iron bridge). The track then curves round to the right to the Attercliffe stop. This serves the Technology Park on the left, a city council-sponsored development project, and the headquarters of Yorkshire Cable, the company with a cable-TV franchise for the area. A new footbridge was built over the canal as part of the scheme, crossing Shirland Lane the line continues on an embankment alongside the canal and crosses Worksop Road on a new bridge. There are three bridges side by side here for there are also the bridge which carries the former Great Central Railway route from Sheffield to Doncaster via Rotherham Central and an aqueduct carrying the canal.

We now see the Don Valley Stadium on our left. This, together with the Arena were both new projects which were developed for the World Student Games (Universiade) in 1991. We now run alongside the aforementioned railway line all the way to Tinsley. The line is used for freight trip workings to the UES works at Stocksbridge, Railfreight Distribution services to and from Aldwarke and light engines to and from Tinsley depot. It is also used for diversionary purposes when the main ex-Midland Railway route from Sheffield to Rotherham is blocked by engineering work and for occasional football specials to Wadsley Bridge, the station near to the Sheffield Wednesday football ground at Hillsborough. This ground will, of course, also be served by South Yorkshire Supertram. Because of the requirement for a large number of sidings associated with the former steelworks along this route, the trackbed is quite wide, and there is room for three tracks, two SYSL and one BR. There are two stations on this section, the first one being Don Valley Stadium/Arena. This station opened after the others as the requirements for handling large crowds at Sports Grounds occasioned by the Taylor Report on safety at sports grounds had not been met by the time the line opened. The other station, Carbrook is behind the "Meadowhall Retail Park" which, despite its name, is not at Meadowhall.

We follow the BR line as far as Tinsley South Junction, where we turn west, utilising the alignment of the former Great Central Railway (later LNER) Barnsley branch alongside the M1 Tinsley Viaduct. Just before crossing the River Don we come across the first of the two stations which serve the Meadowhall complex. This is known as "Meadowhall South/ Tinsley" and is just across the road from the House of Fraser and Debenham's department stores. This station will also be convenient for future leisure developments planned in the area. At Alsing Road, the site of the former BR Tinsley West Junction, our two tracks combine into one before we turn south-west to run alongside the main BR Sheffield-Rotherham railway line and terminate at the Meadowhall Interchange, adjacent to the Meadowhall shopping complex. This Interchange already consisted of a 16-stand bus station and a four-platform railway station and cost £9.2 million.

The gradients on the Meadowhall line are generally not so severe. There are stretches of 1 in 20 in the Parkway–Nunnery area, plus a 150 metre stretch at 1 in 12.5 where the line crosses the railway and drops down onto Woodburn Road, but from Technology Park to Meadowhall Interchange the maximum gradient is 1 in 62 (almost level by light rail standards!).

Above: The busy terminus at Meadowhall Interchange. *Peter Fox*

TRAMSTOPS

Above: A typical stop on ballasted track at Cricket Inn Road *Peter Fox*

Below: The Cathedral stop. Note the patterned concrete surface between the tracks. *Peter Fox*

A total of 45 tram stops, plus a staff halt, are being constructed for the Supertram network. These are generally 26.5 m long and around 3.0 m wide. They are designed to a standard arrangement making them easy to understand and use.

The design incorporates the recommendations of the Cranfield Institute of Technology which was commissioned by South Yorkshire PTE to study platform ergonomics for both able-bodied and mobility-impaired passengers.

Approach ramps with a 1:20 slope provide access to the platforms which are elevated 375 mm above rail level to facilitate level access on to the trams. The platform edge comprises a 600 mm wide, light coloured, textured paving strip with 400 mm wide edge warning tactile strip located to its rear. Directional guidance tactile paving is located across the width of the platform to coincide with the tram door locations.

The platform furniture comprising shelter, ticket purchase and validating machines, lighting, signage, and, where required, fencing to the rear has been designed to provide a consistent 'Supertram' quality image.

Left: Tactile paving on the platform so that blind people know where the edge is and where the tram doors will be. *Peter Fox*

TICKETS & FARES

Above: A bank of machines at a stop. There are two blue ticket machines with a yellow validating machine between them. *Peter Fox*

Buying a ticket to travel on the Supertram system is very easy. At present, each stop has blue ticket machines which dispense Adult single ride tickets for 50p, £1 and in some cases £1.50, senior citizen concessionary tickets at 25p and child concessionary tickets at 15p. The concessionary ticket holders must also hold the necessary South Yorkshire PTE permit and these are only available to residents of South Yorkshire. Diagrams on the stops and fare tables in the leaflets describe the validity of the different prices.

Ticket agencies, for example the PTE Travel Information offices and numerous retail shops such as newsagents, also sell tickets with the adult single tickets being at a discount. Multi-pack purchases give greater discounts, so that at present ten £1 tickets cost £7.50 and ten £1.50 tickets cost £11.50. There is also a weekly ticket at £10 and the SYPTE Railmaster and Travelmaster passes are also valid.

To travel, the ticket from whichever source it was purchased must be validated in the yellow machine on the station platform, before entering the vehicle. The ticket is not valid until this has been done. The passenger then has 90 minutes to complete the single journey. Those with SYPTE passes and SYSL weekly tickets have no time limit, of course.

The machines have been provided by Abberfield Technology of Australia.

The print on the ticket from the machine denotes the type of passenger and trip/concession, the time and date of issue and the code of the tramstop from where the purchase was made, whilst the agency bought ticket shows the retail agent code and machine number in place of the tramstop code. On validation a further print is added showing the tramstop code, time and date of validation.

A warning - Any passenger found travelling without a valid ticket or permit can be charged a penalty fare of £10. Inspection staff will check tickets and an Act of Parliament is held to enforce this charge. Hopefully this will provide sufficient deterrent to those who attempt this anti-social act.

The above fares are those pertaining at the time of writing, but it should be noted that they are subject to change at any time.

Note: Unlike most British bus tickets, Supertram tickets are valid for a break of journey or change of vehicle within the time limit. Thus one can travel from Gleadless Townend to Fitzalan Square and then change onto a Meadowhall tram as far as Carbrook for £1 (or 75p if as multi-pack has been purchased). Alternatively the trip from Manor Top/Elm Tree to Meadowhall would cost the same fare.

A close-up of a ticket machine. *Peter Fox*

Above: A ticket issued as part of a pack of ten tickets. Note the '75p' price.

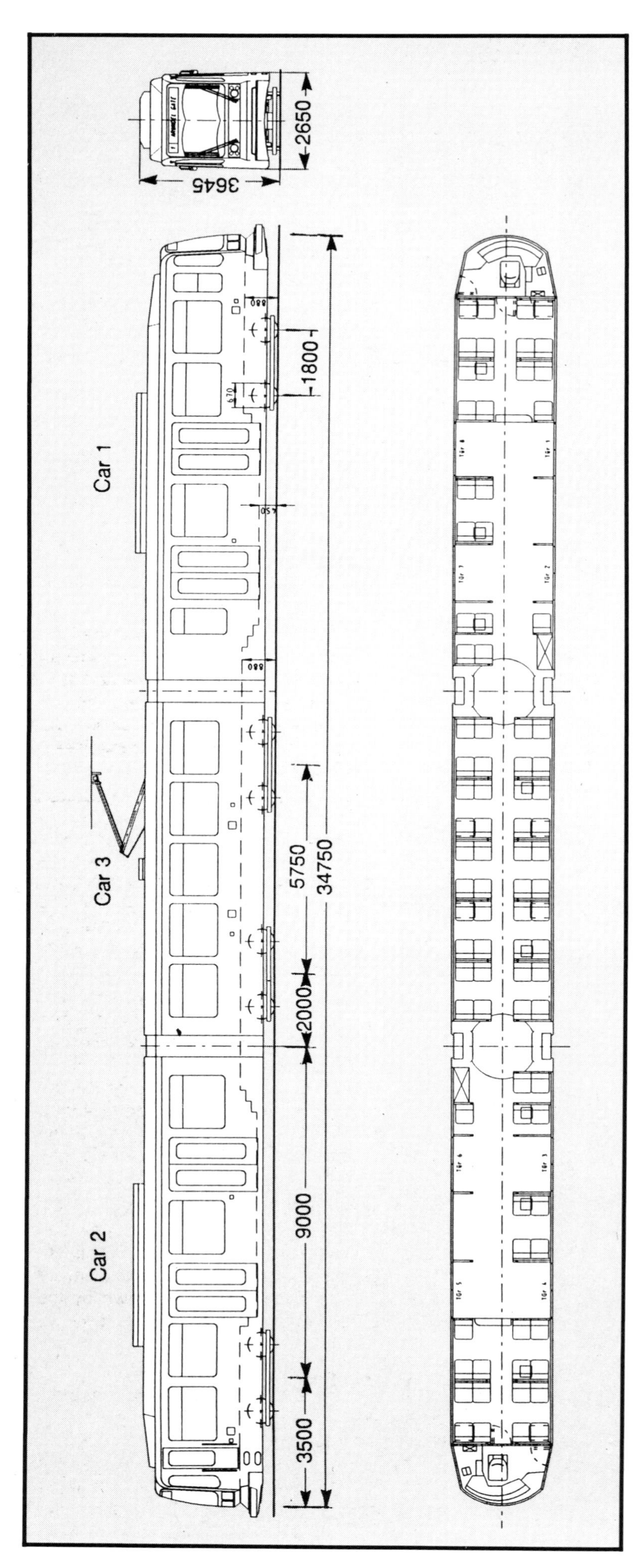

Left: General view of a South Yorkshire Supertram (measurements in mm). *Siemens*

Below: Tram No. 02 at the Rheinbahn depot in Düsseldorf before delivery to Sheffield. The tram carried the number 1002 allocated by the Rheinbahn for use when on trials on their system. *South Yorkshire Supertram Ltd.*

THE TRAMS

The trams were delivered to Sheffield by road from the makers Siemens-Duewag in Düsseldorf, Germany, via the Rotterdam-Immingham ferry. Initially, certain of them underwent trials on the Rheinbahn system in Düsseldorf. They are bi-directional cars with a 40% low-floor area. All entrances are at the low level (420 mm at the doors) which matches the height of the platforms, thus ensuring level access. There is then, in the low-floor area, a gentle slope up to the height of 480 mm, where there is limited seating together with space for prams, wheel chairs etc. The high floor areas, 880 mm high, are at the outer end of each of the outer sections, and in the centre section, these are reached by either two or three steps.

Since the Sheffield system has gradients as steep as 10%, the car had to have all axles powered. This effectively limited the low-floor area to that between the bogies. By arranging the two centre bogies so that they are entirely under the centre section and not under the articulation, the low-floor area was maximised. The tram wheels (type Bochum 84) have resilient rubber inserts and have a diameter of 670 mm that can be worn to a diameter of 590 mm.

The futuristic driver's cab. *SYSL*

Control is by a proven technology d.c. chopper system with GTO semiconductors. It is possible to do without braking series resistors as a result of a suitable motor design, which brings considerable regenerative energy savings during braking. There are four longitudinal d.c. fully suspended monomotors which drive both axles in each bogie.

Special importance has been placed on the tram exterior design to achieve a pleasing appearance in the city scene and also on the trams's interior, the fittings and colour scheme of which have been selected, after market research, to suit the requirements of the users.

The vehicle interior has been designed from an aesthetic point of view and to meet stringent safety requirements. The interior fittings have no sharp edges to prevent any injury to passengers or to the operating and maintenance staff during normal operation and also in emergencies. Particular emphasis has been placed on providing passengers with sufficient holding possibilities.

The interior lining for the ceiling consists of an aluminium honeycomb design, to which coloured melamine resin panels have been bonded. The lining is attached to suspension points welded to the roof section. The inside walls are made of coloured melamine material. The complete lining for the articulations consists of coloured fibre-glass reinforced plastic. The rear wall of the driving cab is made of laminated wood with a melamine veneer.

The vehicle has 88 comfortable seats arranged face to face. In the low-floor areas in sections 1 and 2, space is provided for wheelchairs directly adjacent to the doors. The dimensions of the wheelchair areas and the passages to them are in accordance with the requirements laid down by the Disabled Persons Transport Advisory Committee (DPTAC) in the United Kingdom.

Great emphasis has been given to the accessibility of the vehicles for those in wheelchairs. Extensive studies were completed by the Cranfield Institute of Technology to ensure this important section of the public be particularly catered for. It is an obvious fact that any benefit provided for the disabled brings undoubted benefits for all, especially parents with pushchairs etc. *Photo SYSL*

THE TRACK

The Sheffield system features two types of track -tramway track where either pedestrians or road vehicles need to share the right of way and ballasted railway track where there is no such requirement.

Tramway Track

Tramway track consists of a grooved tramway rail set into a concrete base with troughs into which the rails are laid. In order to carry out the building of the street track in the shortest possible time Balfour Beatty, the main contractors, decided to use a slip-form paver to produce this concrete base. Slip-form pavers have been used for many jobs in the past, e.g. roads, kerbs, airport runways, but this is the first time that one has been used for tramway construction.

The process starts with the delivery of ready-mixed concrete which has been pre-mixed to a specified tolerance. Having first tested a sample of the concrete, it is then poured from the lorry onto a conveyor which feeds onto a screw. This screw forces the concrete, via a series of vibrating pokers, under the body of the machine to the steel formwork which produces the grooved concrete. This is then hand-floated and brushed to provide an anti-skid surface. It is then sprayed with an aluminium-resin curing agent. The operation requires a 6 m^3 lorry-load every 6 linear metres and the process produces around 250 metres in an 8 hour day. This compares with the 50-100 m/day which would be achieved using formwork shuttering. When paving is interrupted, it is not possible to continue from where the laying stopped, and the gap left has to be filled in. This is because it is not possible to fit the former into the groove after it has dried.

After four or five days it is possible to lay the grooved tramway rail. This is first laid on top of the concrete slab and is made into a solid mass by sticking 400 mm long pre-formed concrete blocks into the web. These are glued using an adhesive compatible with the polymer into which the rails will later be set. The purpose of these blocks is to prevent rail web oscillation and hence provide a quiet ride. The rails are welded together using the "Thermit" process, before being cross-bonded for electrical purposes. During the paving operation, pipes are laid so that bonding wire can be placed through and Cad-welded to the rail webs before these are placed in the grooves. The next stage is to pack the bottom and side of the concrete groove for alignment every metre, drop in the rail and pour in the Edilon polymer in two stages - neat to above the rail foot and dilute between the foot and the surface.

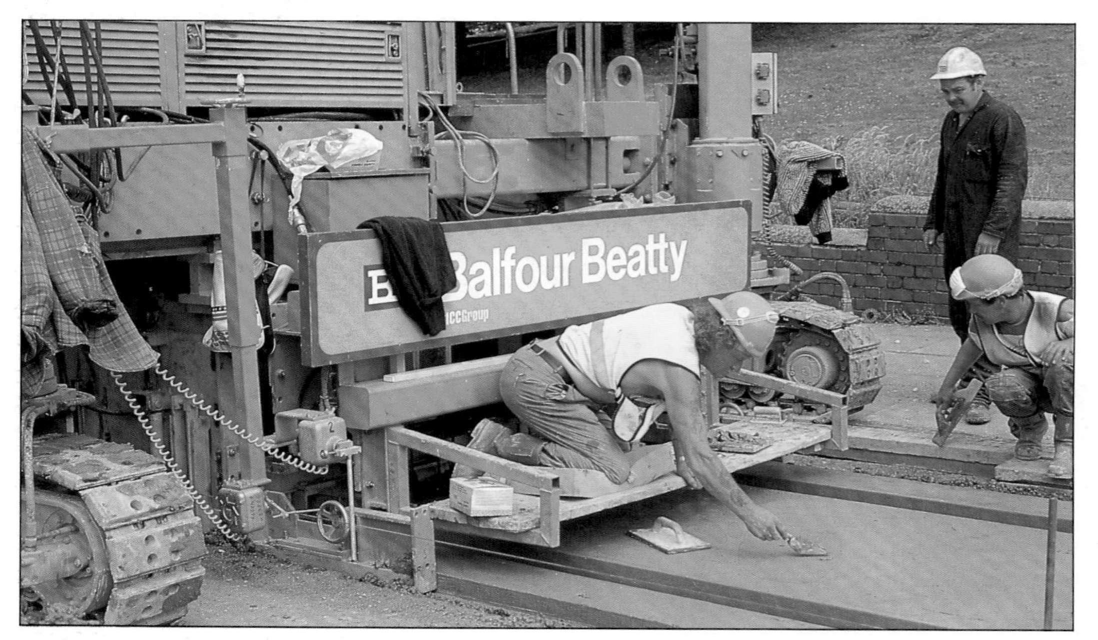

Left: A slip-former in use on City Road producing the concrete base into which the rails will be laid. The operative is manually trowelling the surface as the machine progresses along the road. *Peter Fox*

Right: Tramway rails laid on top of the concrete base on the street crossing on Woodbourn Road. This piece of track was the first one to be produced with tramway rail. *Peter Fox*

Left: The concrete base as produced by the slip-former, this time on Park Grange Road. The steel reinforcement can be seen protruding from the end. *Peter Fox*

Right: Rails waiting to be laid into the troughing. Concrete blocks are affixed to the webs to reduce the amount of polymer which needs to be used to set the rails in the troughs in the trackbed. *Peter Fox*

Railway Track

Railway track consists of BS11 - 80A 80 lb/yd flat-bottomed rail, supplied by British Steel Track Products of Workington, laid on sleepers consisting of concrete blocks with steel ties. The track is laid on a bed of ballast which in turn rests on a prepared formation. Street crossings in areas of railway track may either be laid in railway rail with a steel section alongside to provide an edge for the concrete, or with grooved tramway rails.

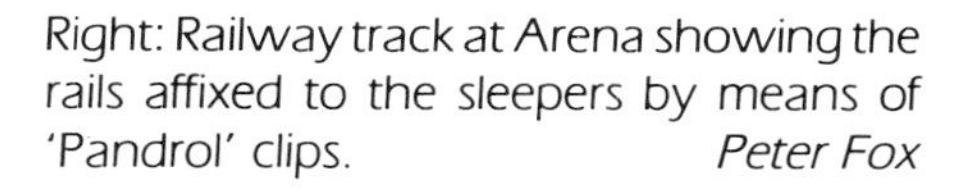

Right: Railway track at Arena showing the rails affixed to the sleepers by means of 'Pandrol' clips. *Peter Fox*

OPERATION

The operation of a light rail system is a complex affair. In some respects the rules are similar to those of a conventional railway, but in other respects they differ from this, especially when operating in the street or at tram stops where pedestrians cross on the level and therefore have right of way. The system is operated by the South Yorkshire Supertram Operating Company (SYSOC). This company is in effect a sub-contractor and operates the depot and employs all the operating staff.

Staff

The staff which actually operate the trams are known as 'customer service agents' (CSAs). These people can drive the trams and can also be employed as ticket inspectors. Thus the same person can be checking tickets and assisting passengers one week and on driving duties the week after. There are also a number of driver's supervisors who carry out training duties etc.

Signalling System

Unlike a normal train, a tram is versatile enough to be able to operate without signals, although in some cases block signalling (as on the railway) is necessary, for example to ensure that trams do not collide on a single-line section. On the South Yorkshire Supertram system, the normal method of operation is that of driving on-sight, i.e. the speed of the tram is such that the tram can stop with normal service brakes if an obstruction is spotted on the track ahead. Consideration was originally given to the fitting of block signalling (known as 'safety signalling' by SYSL) on the segregated section of line between Attercliffe and Meadowhall, but this was found unnecessary.

Below: A warning sign on City Road telling drivers what to do if they do not receive a 'proceed' indication from the signal on the right above the road traffic lights. *Peter Fox*

Above: A warning signal for pedestrians by the Woodbourn Road stop. *Peter Fox*

Signals are however necessary to give indications to tram drivers when running on-street and at street crossings. Because trams have priority at many places, it is necessary to give them different traffic light phases from motor traffic and therefore different types of indication have to be used from those applicable to motor vehicles. Thus it has been decided that trams shall not obey the normal red/amber/green traffic lights, but will have their own signals which consist of white lights arranged vertically (for go) or horizontally (for stop). There is also a cross which is the tram equivalent of the normal amber road signal. There are other signals which show point indications at junctions.

At present, safety signalling is only used to protect single-line sections, e.g. between Alsing Road and Meadowhall. For consistency the same light indications are used as on non-safety tram signals.

Lineside Signs

Lineside signs give instructions or warnings to tram drivers. To distinguish them from normal road signs they are diamond-shaped. The most common signs are speed restriction signs which are in miles per hour (the United Kingdom shows no sign of metricating its traffic rules!). These are necessary as trams sometimes have more severe speed restrictions on street than motor traffic Also on partially segregated tracks trams can run at higher speeds than road vehicles. Whereas motor traffic tends to adjust its speed in the light of circumstances as perceived by the driver, trams have the speed imposed by the speed restriction signs which have to be agreed with the railway inspectorate. Other signs give various types of warning or information and these are shown in the diagram.

As well as signs for tram drivers there are also warning signs for other road users, i.e. driverrs and pedestrians.

Routing

The route which a tram is to take is computer-controlled. The route is set on a device in the tram before a journey is commenced, and on the approach to junctions a signal is sent from the tram to a device known as a VIS loop buried beneath the track. This then automatically sets the points for the correct direction. The driver knows that the correct direction has been set by observing a lineside direction signal. This is necessary in case of failure of the apparatus. The driver can also operate the points by sending a signal to the VIS loop. Some points are sprung so that they automatically return to one setting, and because they have no locking apparatus they can be pushed over by the tram's wheels when operating in a trailing direction. The VIS system also operates where a tram stop is in advance of traffic signals and in such cases is used by the driver to tell the traffic light computer that the tram is ready to depart. A good example of this is at Attercliffe where the station is just in advance of the Shirland Lane traffic lights

Stopping at Tram Stops

The present policy is that all normal service cars will stop at all stops en route, but if a passenger wishes to alight, he or she must press the 'request to stop' button. If this is not done, the driver will not enable the doors to be opened. If this button is pressed before the tram stops, it must be pressed again once the tram has come to a stop in order to open the particular set of doors at which the passenger wishes to alight.

SUPERTRAM SIGNALS & INDICATORS

FIXED SIGNALS

Signals normally display five white lights which are distinctive from those of the standard road traffic lights or railway lineside signals and have the meanings indicated:

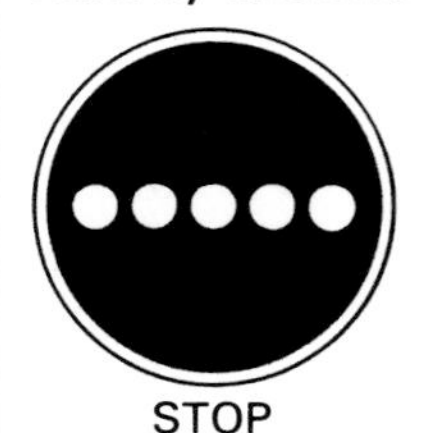

STOP

STRAIGHT THROUGH TRAM OR TRAIN MAY PROCEED

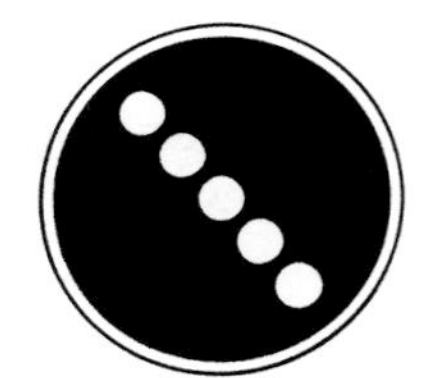

LEFT TURNING TRAM OR TRAIN MAY PROCEED

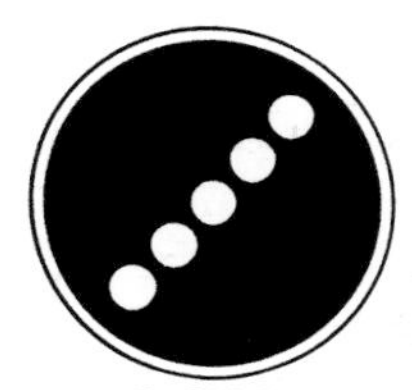

RIGHT TURNING TRAM OR TRAIN MAY PROCEED

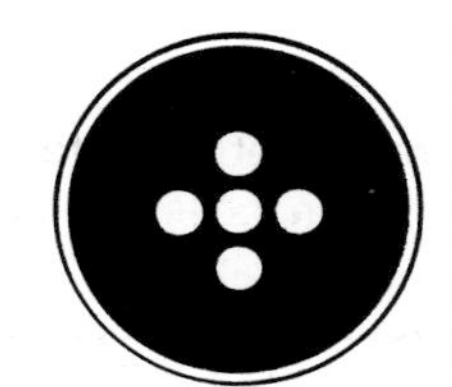

THIS IS EQUIVALENT TO AN AMBER ROAD TRAFFIC LIGHT SIGNAL

POINTS INDICATORS

Points indicators are provided at junctions to indicate the route which is set through points. At junctions where the tram and train movements can conflict with road traffic, fixed signals are provided in addition to points indicators. The aspects displayed by the points indicators are:

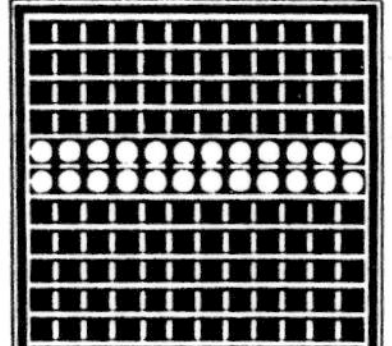

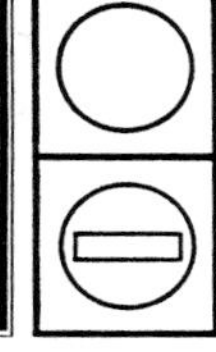

STOP (POINTS MISALIGNED/NOT DETECTED)

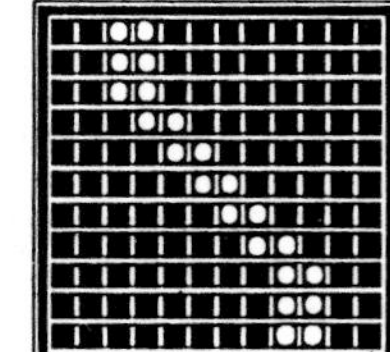

POINTS SET FOR LEFT TURNING TRACK

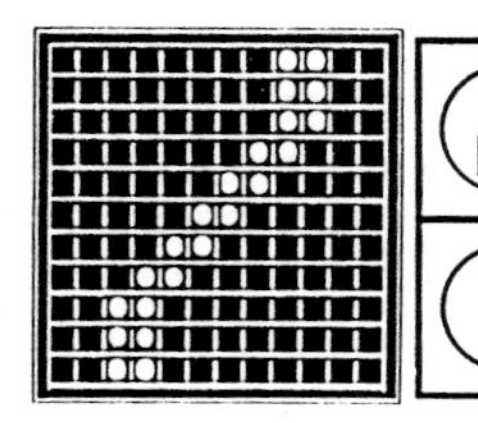

POINTS SET FOR RIGHT TURNING TRACK

A points indicator may be passed only if it displays the correct route indication for the tram or train concerned and, where fixed signals are provided, if both points indicators and fixed signals are set for the correct route.

SUPERTRAM SIGNS

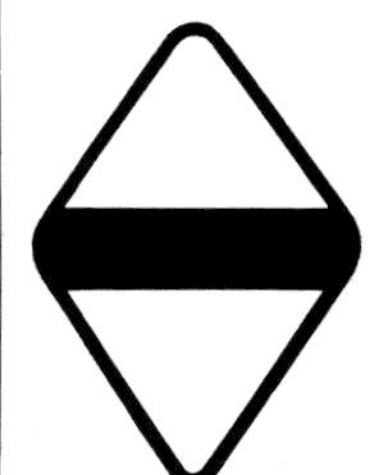

STOP AND PROCEED WHEN SAFE TO DO SO

GIVE WAY TO ANOTHER TRAM, TRAIN OR ROAD VEHICLE

MAXIMUM PERMITTED SPEED IN MILES PER HOUR

SOUND AUDIBLE WARNING

TEMPORARY SPEED RESTRICTION

TERMINATION OF TEMPORARY SPEED RESTRICTION

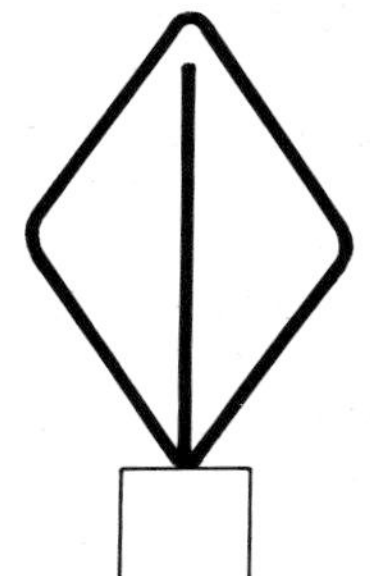

INSTRUCTION SIGN. OBSERVE SPECIFIC INSTRUCTION ON PLATE BELOW

EXAMPLES OF SPECIFIC INSTRUCTIONS

S — PREPARE TO STOP AT COMMENCEMENT POINT OF INTERLOCKING AREA

SS — INTERLOCKING AREA COMMENCES (''SAFETY SIGNALLING'')

TERMINATION OF INTERLOCKING AREA

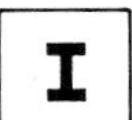

SECTION GAP

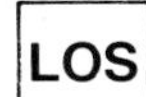

LIMIT OF SHUNT

NUNNERY DEPOT

Above: The depot from Woodbourn Road. *Peter Fox*

The depot, situated at Nunnery close to the city centre, has been designed and constructed by Balfour Beatty on 2.6 hectares of land and consists of a three-line workshop building, 6 stabling sidings, a turning loop, engineers sidings and sundry equipment. The main offices and reception, supervisor's offices, plant room, staff mess rooms, paint shop, first aid etc. are on the first floor level on the south side of the structure. The south west corner on this level houses the nerve centre of the whole scheme, this is the Operations and Power Controller's office, where minute by minute control of the running of the service is monitored using SCADA, CCTV and radio contact. The depot sub station is also located on the south west corner, providing power to operate the trams and internal depot supply. Two 600 kVA transformer-rectifiers supply the tramway overhead and a single 800 kVA transformer feeds the depot necessities. All operations and maintenance personnel work from this site. To the south, immediately outside the building, on the main running line, is to be found the Nunnery crew change tram stop.

Within the workshop itself, two lines (Nos. 8 and 9) are through running, whilst No. 10 is stub end. All lines have inspection pits, the one on line 8 housing the Hegenscheidt wheel lathe. This machine is located in the centre of the shed and this allows wheel turning to take place whilst both sets of outer doors are closed. The wheelsets are turned in situ, i.e. they do not have to be removed from the tram. High level access to vehicle roofs is possible between lines 9 and 10 for servicing equipment boxes and pantographs. Sanding apparatus is also installed by these two lines. In addition a 6 tonne travelling crane installed. On line 7, outside on the north side of the building is the automatic washing machine and the sand hopper. The workshop is painted in a very attractive mixture of blue, red and yellow. Each evening after service, the cars will pass through the workshop for daily inspection, pass through the washer and be stabled on one of the stabling sidings (numbered 1 to 6).

Vehicles can leave or enter the depot from either the east or west gates, the east exit being up a very steep gradient to the running line by Woodbourn Road. The west end of the site provides a head shunt for depot stabling without causing problems with the main line running signals.

Security on the site is of the highest standard. CCTV cameras, fence guarding equipment etc. being under the control of security personnel housed in the Operations centre. Road access is from Woodbourn Road at the east end of the complex.

It should be noted here that before the Supertram depot was built on the site, this area had already served the railway industry. The whole location had seen tracks of the Midland, Great Central and London & North Western Railways together with the Nunnery Colliery Co. An engine shed belonging to the LNWR was on part of this site and the building existed until the late 1960s.

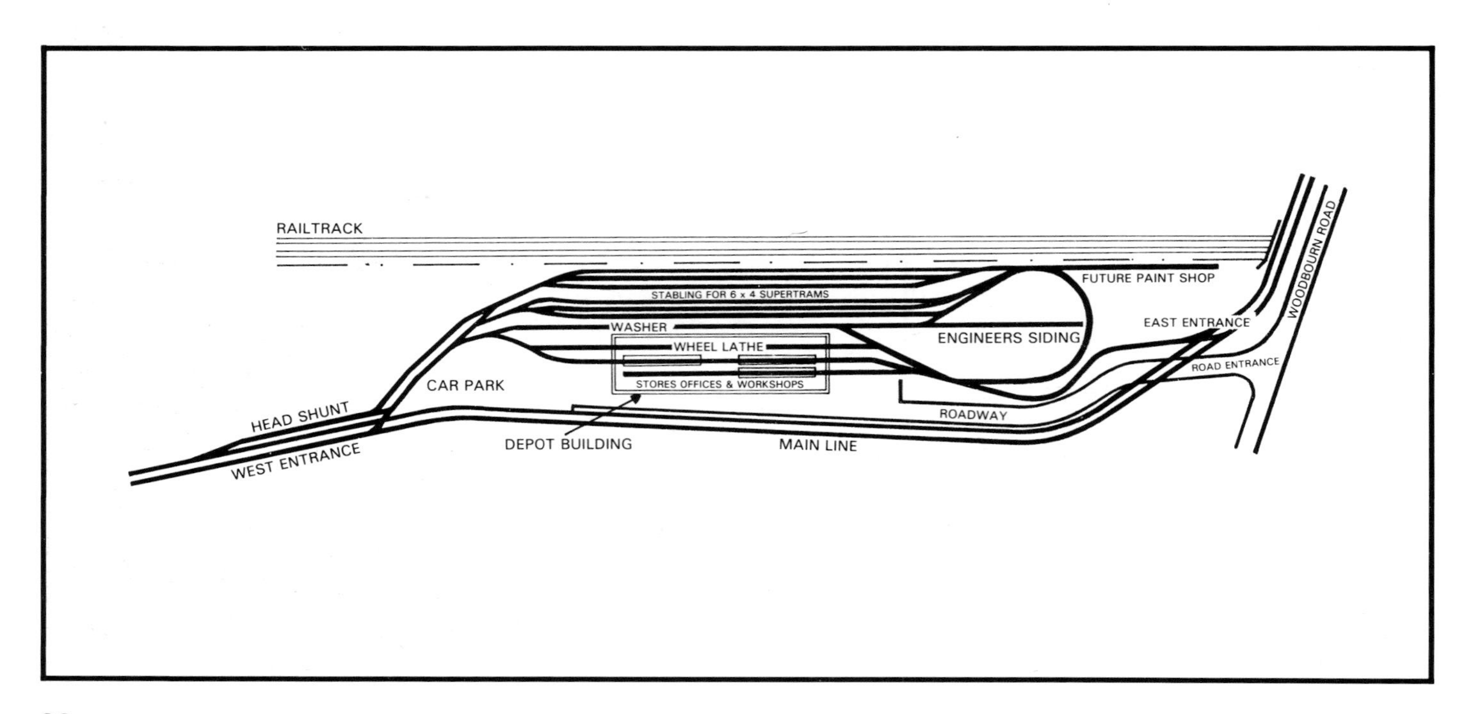

Views inside the depot. The top photo is a general view, whilst the photo below shows the bogie storage area. On the right is the Hegenscheidt wheel lathe. *Peter Fox*

Left: A diagram of the track layout in the depot area.

Right: A new tram being unloaded from the delivery lorry in the depot *SYSL*

POWER SUPPLY

The trams take their power from overhead line equipment (OHLE) and this in turn receives its current from substations. The sub-stations convert the 11 kV a.c. supply into the 750 V d.c. supply for the overhead. There are 12 sub-stations as follows:

Blackburn Meadows
Carbrook
Nunnery
Park Square
Arbourthorne
Gleadless (Ridgeway Road - behind No. 153)
Birley
Crystal Peaks (Ochre Dyke Lane)
Halfway (Eckington Way)
University (south-west corner near Brook Hill and Upper Hanover Street)
Langsett Road (on the corner of Capel Street)
Middlewood

Above: Overhead line equipment on Park Grange Road. *Peter Fox*

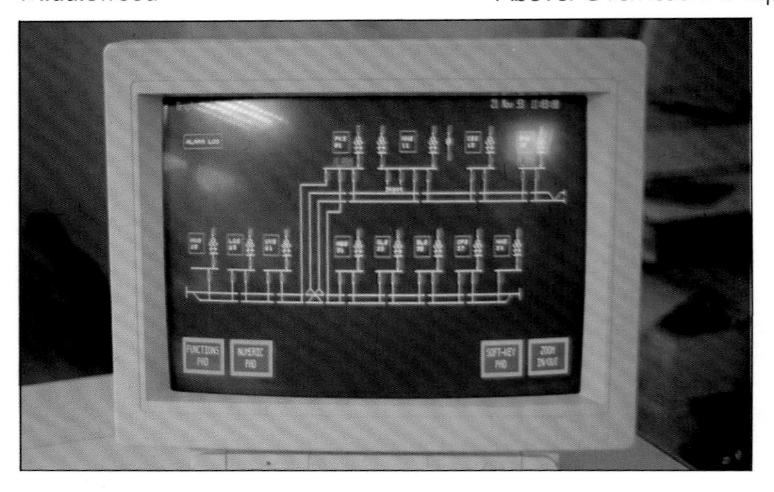

Above: The power controller's diagram in the depot control room. *Peter Fox*

Overhead Line Equipment

The overhead line equipment used depends on the location of the tracks. If the two tracks are close together, as on most of the Meadowhall route, a central pole is used with arms on each side. Where the tracks are further apart as on Park Grange Road there are poles on either side with span wires between them. In the City Centre building fixings have been used wherever possible to obviate the need for poles.

The contact wires are twin Cadmium Copper ones, twin wires being necessary because of the high installed power rating of the Siemens trams (1 Megawatt). The equipment is not only used for powering the trams. The regenerative braking on the trams actually feeds current back into the wires in a similar way to the electric locomotives which worked the now-closed Woodhead line between Manchester and Sheffield. Part of what is now the Meadowhall route was formerly used by these locomotives when working freight trains to Tinsley Yard.

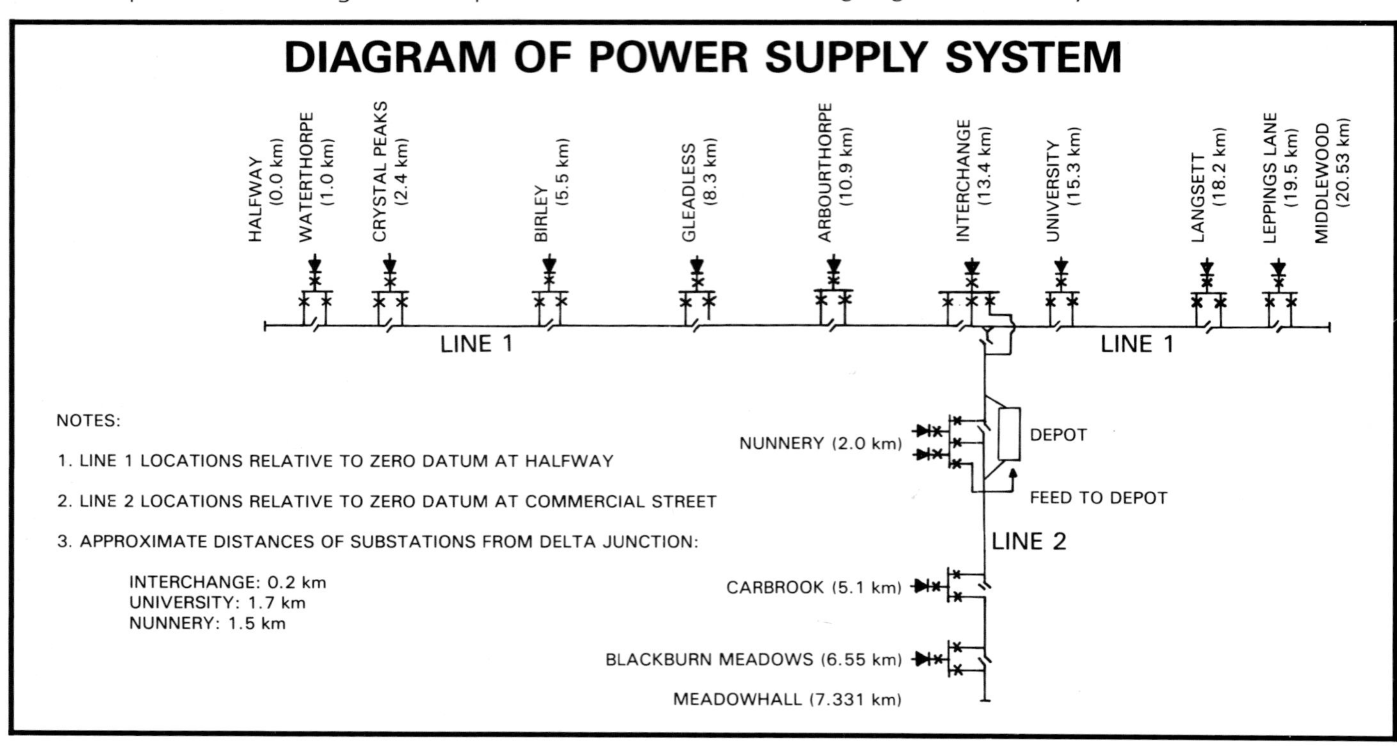

Sheffield Tramway Pictorial

Right: South Yorkshire Supertram Ltd. are now running trams through Sheffield City Centre along a similar path to that taken by Sheffield's old trams. On the second day of public operation to the Cathedral, Sunday 19th February 1995, tram 13 runs up High Street past C & A with Fitzalan Square in the background.
Peter Fox

Right: A busy street scene at the junction of Haymarket and Commercial Street in September 1959 . Two Roberts cars and one domed-roof car can be seen. Note the policeman on point duty, something hardly ever seen these days.
Bernard Mettam

Below: Spectators returning home from the Don Valley Stadium after the MacDonald's games (athletics) on 4th September 1994 found supertram a convenient and comfortable mode of transport.
Paul Jackson

TRAMS THEN . . . . .

Left: domed-roof car No. 242 heading for Crookes runs up Church Street towards West Street on a peak-hour special from Brightside on 4th May 1957. *Bernard Mettam*

Right: At the same spot on 12th March 1995 a Gleadless-Shalesmoor Supertram follows a similar path. The buildings in the left foreground have been replaced, but all other buildings still exist. *Peter Fox*

Above: Looking towards West Street on the same two dates Standard car No. 210 in new livery is seen in the picture on the left on a Crookes-Handsworth working *(Bernard Mettam))* whilst on the right a Supertram runs along the newly-laid track. Because of the right-turning lane for vehicular traffic, this eastbound track is much further to the left then the original tram track *(Peter Fox)*.

AND NOW

Below: City Road at its junction with Wilfric Road. On 11th February 1956 (left) standard car No. 124 in old livery on a working to Intake and Darnall via Prince of Wales Road *(Bernard Mettam))*. On 12th March 1995 (right) a Shalesmoor-Gleadless Supertram passes the same houses, albeit renovated with new windows and satellite dishes *(Peter Fox))*.

SUPERTRAMS IN ROTHERHAM, DERBYSHIRE AND THE HEART OF SHEFFIELD

Left: **A Supertram in Rotherham**. A short section of single line between Meadowhall Interchange and Alsing Road crossing is in Rotherham although there are no stops there. Well-loaded Supertram No. 13 can be seen with the BR Midland Main Line in the background and the Meadowhall car park in the foreground. A Supertram route to Rotherham is under study by South Yorkshire Passenger Transport Executive. *Peter Fox*

Below Left: **A Supertram in Derbyshire**. The section of line from the end of White Lane through to Birley Lane is actually in North-East Derbyshire, although again no stops are involved. Tram 08 is seen on a trial run from Gleadless Townend to Halfway on 6th March 1995. Derbyshire County Council have decided to support extensions of light rail schemes into Derbyshire as part of their new 'Transport Policies and programmes' document. *Peter Fox*

Below: **The Heart of the System**. A Gleadless-bound tram leaves the triangular track layout at Park Square on 12th February 1995. On the left of the picture is the bowstring arch bridge carrying tracks leading to Sheffield City Centre and to the right are the tracks leading to Meadowhall. *Peter Fox*

TIMES & SEASONS

Right: On a bright summer's day Supertram 05 runs across South Street Bridge towards Granville Street behind Sheffield Midland Station with a driver-training run to Spring Lane. *Les Nixon*

Left: The snowfall of 23rd February 1994 saw Sheffield's traffic in a mess, but the trams, then not yet in public service, kept going. A Supertram runs off the bowstring arch bridge towards Commercial Street.
Duncan Anderson

Right: Evening sunlight on the new bridge over the Sheffield Canal between Attercliffe and Woodbourn Road as a Meadowhallto Cathedral tram crosses.
Peter Fox:

TRAMS IN THE 50s

Above: A depot-bound domed-roof car runs along Sheaf Street in front of Sheffield Midland station on 19th September 1959. In the background Park Hill Flats are under construction, but much of the terraced housing is still standing. *Bernard Mettam*

Left: A busy time on 7th November 1952 at Moorhead with the old 'Nelson' public house in the background. On the inbound track is a 1928 standard car bound for Holme Lane, whilst on the outbound track are three similar cars bound for Millhouses, Ecclesall and Millhouses & Abbey Lane respectively. *R B Parr courtesy National Tramway Museum*

Below: A Crookes-bound tram runs past the old Corn Exchange on 4th May 1957. The Park Square roundabout now occupies this site. *Bernard Mettam*

Above: London Road at Heeley Bottom on 13th July 1952 with Meadowhead-Sheffield Lane Top route trams seen running in both directions. The track from Queens Road runs in to the right and on the left can be seen an enthusiast's special working coming out of Wolseley Road. *R.B. Parr courtesy National Tramway Museum*

Right: Wolseley Road did not have regular workings but was used for storing trams during Sheffield United football matches at nearby Bramall Lane. No less than twelve trams are seen on 22nd August 1957. Gaps are left at strategic intervals for pedestrians to cross. *R. B. Parr courtesy National Tramway Museum*

Below: Standard car 191 in new livery rounds the corner at Beauchief with an Abbey Lane Circular working during 1954 bound for Sheffield Lane Top. *LRTA Frank Hunt Collection*

Above: Supertram 24 on Ridgeway Road approaching Gleadless Townend. Some of the track on Ridgeway Road is on reservation, but some of it is on the outside lane of the dual carriageway. *Peter Fox*

Below Left: The last of the 25 Supertrams being delivered from Germany on the M180 in what is at present called "Humberside" *Duncan Anderson*

Below Right: Parkway Central park and ride. This is a new PTE-owned car park just off the Sheffield Parkway road and adjacent to Cricket Inn Road tram stop. The £2 charge includes the return tram fare as far as the University of Sheffield. *Peter Fox*

Some Recommended Reading on Sheffield's old Tramway System

SHEFFIELD TRANSPORT C.C. Hall. Transport Publishing Company 1977 (out of print).

SHEFFIELD CORPORATION TRAMWAYS Kenneth Gandy. Sheffield City Libraries 1985 (out of print).

SHEFFIELD TRAMS REMEMBERED Graham Hague & Howard Turner. Sheaf Publishing1987.

ACKNOWLEDGEMENTS

The authors and publisher would like to acknowledge the help received from the South Yorkshire Passenger Transport Executive, South Yorkshire Supertram Ltd., Balfour Beatty Power Constuction Ltd, the National Tramway Museum, the Light Rail Transit Association, Bernard Mettam, R.J.S. Wiseman, Duncan Anderson and all other individuals or companies who have helped in any way.

UK LIGHT RAIL SYSTEMS No. 2

Readers may be interested to know that a more comprehensive book about the South Yorkshire Supertram System will be published towards the end of 1995 or in the early part of 1996. This book, No. 2 in our UK Light Rail Systems series, will deal in detail with the political, technical, commercial and operational aspects of the system. Please see announcements nearer the time in 'Today's Railways', 'Light Rail and Modern Tramway' or 'Light Rail Review 7'. Please note that No. 1 in this series 'Manchester Metrolink' is at present out of print, but a reprint will be available shortly.

FRONT COVER: Commercial Street seen from Park Hill flats with a Supertram heading towards Gleadless *(Peter Fox)*. Most buildings on the right hand side of the road are unchanged since the 50s, although the gas offices in the foreground are at present disused. The left hand side of the road is, however, new as all buildings were demolished when the road was widened in the 60s. The inset *(Bernard Mettam))* shows 'Roberts' car No. 516 on a Millhouses-Vulcan Road working coming down High Street on 3rd July 1960. Tram tracks once again occupy this space and the infamous 'hole in the road' has been and gone since this picture was taken.

BACK COVER: Top: Trams pass one another on Park Grange Road on a snowy January day in 1995. *Peter Fox*

Bottom: The beautifully restored short canopy double-deck car No. 74 at the National Tramway Museum, Crich, Derbyshire, Summer 1994. *National Tramway Museum*